RAVEN TALES

RAVEN TALES

selected and edited by

PETER GOODCHILD

CHICAGO REVIEW PRESS

Library of Congress Cataloging-in-Publication Data

Goodchild, Peter.
    The raven tales / Peter Goodchild.
        p.   cm.
    Includes bibliographical references (p.   ) and index.
    ISBN 1-55652-100-6 (cloth) : $16.95. — ISBN 1-55652-101-4
    (pbk.) $9.95
    1. Indians of North America—Northwest Coast of North
America--Legends. 2. Ravens—Folklore. I. Title.
E78.N78G66   1991
398.24'528864'08997—dc20   90-27379
                                                CIP

Cover painting: Big Raven ("Cumshewa") by Emily Carr, 1931.
Courtesy of the Vancouver Art Gallery, Vancouver, B.C.

Copyright ©1991 by Peter Goodchild
Published by Chicago Review Press, Chicago
            5 4 3 2 1

Printed in the United States of America

For Sook-Hee

Contents

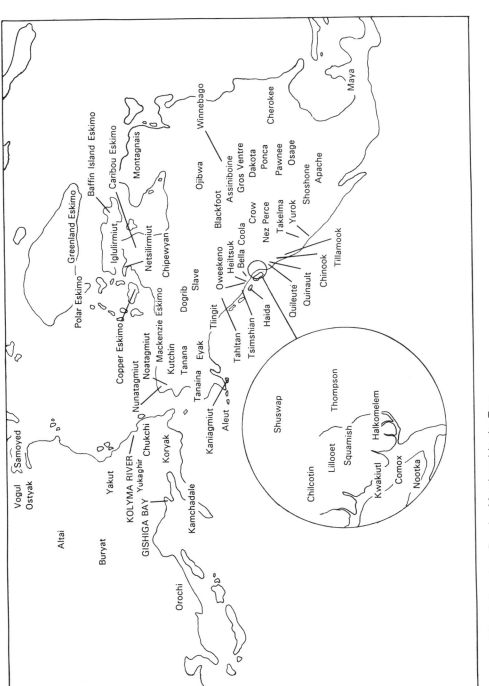

Siberian and North American Peoples Mentioned in the Text

Preface

THE RAVEN TALES ARE A MAJOR ASPECT OF THE NATIVE CULTURE of the Northwest Coast, and yet no full-scale study of them has been published until now. Perhaps the closest to an in-depth study has been Franz Boas' *Tsimshian Mythology*, published in 1916, but that volume only partly deals with the Raven myths, and it is mainly a classification of the tales, not so much a discussion of them.

There are problems with Boas' study. He concentrates on the Tsimshian variants, whereas those of the Tlingit Indians make a better starting point. Like some of his contemporaries, he is careless in translating the names of animals, populating the myths with devilfish, bluebirds, blue jays, tomtits, panthers, and other creatures that have little or no biological meaning in terms of Northwest Coast fauna. Nevertheless, the book is a remarkably inclusive compilation of the recorded versions in the Northwest Coast area.

There are several books that deal specifically with the Tlingit versions of the Raven tales; John Reed Swanton's *Tlingit Myths and Texts* is by far the best compilation.

Waldemar Bogoras, in "The Folklore of Northeastern Asia, as Compared with That of Northwestern America," shows, beyond all question, that the Raven tales of North America and those of eastern Siberia are very similar, and that the two groups of tales must have had a common origin. Waldemar Jochelson, in *Religion and Myths of the Koryak*, also offers a comparative study of Siberian and American myths.

Anna B. Rooth's *The Raven and the Carcass* is a detailed academic study of the motif of the raven that Noah let out of the ark. Her analysis helps us to understand two major myths, that of "The Deluge" and that of "The Earth Diver."

In *The Folklore of Birds*, Edward A. Armstrong makes a number of interesting comments on possible ties between the New World and Old World raven figures, and on northern myths in general.

Particularly in terms of stories other than those of the Northwest Coast, the words "raven" and "crow" can present a semantic problem. The words are used rather interchangeably in English, and the related terms are confused in other languages. In scientific nomenclature, the crows form a genus, *Corvus*, consisting of about forty species. The common raven is one species, *Corvus corax*, a large bird native to most of the Northern Hemisphere. The hooded crow, the carrion crow, the rook, and the jackdaw are four more European species, and the American crow is common in North America. It is *Corvus corax*, however, who plays the part of the Northwest Coast hero. Various "crows" also appear in the myths of many Old World gods. In the case of the Norse god Odin and the Greco-Roman god Apollo, the "crow" in question is known to be the raven.

The tales we shall be looking at are the most popular ones. There are often several recorded versions of each. When the known variants of a story do not differ much, and a brief but coherent printed version of the story exists, that version is quoted below. When that is not the case, we shall be looking at the general form of the story and some of the main variations.

In this volume I am only presenting a few versions of each of the tales, enough to give an approximate idea of the archetype or prototype of the story—or at least the average form, the principal cluster of motifs. Some of the more important differences among the variants are pointed out; for the general reader, these may be more informative than either isolated aberrations or, on the other hand, twenty almost identical versions. For some of the tales, there are far more versions on record than I have presented.

The first chapter includes only the Tlingit variants of the tales, in order to show approximately how the tales would normally be told within one culture. The further variants are easier to comprehend after one has had a chance to examine one complete form of the Raven cycle.

My arrangement of the stories is basically the same as that used by Boas, although I divide them into thirteen "origin tales" and eighteen "trickster tales," whereas he has four groups: "origin tales," "incidents based on raven's voraciousness," "amorous adventures," and "miscellaneous adventures." He also has a list of "explanatory tales contained in the various versions, but occurring only once or twice" ([1916] 1970, 572–81).

The story of Raven's birth is not included in Boas' list, although he later devotes many pages to it ([1916] 1970, 621–39). He has Raven's change of color as three separate stories (nos. 10, 19, and 20), although they consist largely of a single story, i.e., that of "The Painting of the Birds," and one or two incidents that only rate as explanatory elements. Boas places "Cormorant's Tongue Is Pulled Out" after "The Killing of Grizzly Bear," but I have reversed these stories, since it is Raven's actions toward Grizzly Bear that supply the motive for pulling out Cormorant's tongue. Boas also makes the Haida story of the theft of the moon a separate tale, although it is only a variant of "The Theft of the Sun." Finally, four "salmon" stories (his nos. 12–15) seem to be as closely related as the "slave" stories, for example, and should, for the sake of consistency, likewise be listed as one story. I have omitted eight stories from Boas' list because they seem too uncommon, too fragmentary, or otherwise unimportant.

I have treated the stories of "The Origin of Death" as largely equivalent to stories of "The Origin of Humans." The stories of the origin of humans, from one area to another, sometimes have little in common, but the same could be said of the stories of the origin of death—or of several other tales that Boas lists. It is unfortunate that

Boas finds no place in his system for so important an "origin" as that of humans.

But no list can be perfect. There is no way to reduce the tales to a tidy, totally consistent system, because there has never been such a system among the original storytellers. We find what might be called systemization in the way a cause-and-effect link is established among several stories or incidents: the jealous uncle, the deluge, and Raven's voraciousness; the theft of the sun and its release; Grizzly Bear and Cormorant; the "slave" incidents; and so on. Yet even in these cases the cohesion breaks down when one looks at other variants of those tales. The contradictions and inconsistencies of the Raven tales cannot be removed without destroying the stories.

In the following pages, I have tried to present the tales within an orderly framework that encompasses the myths of a number of cultures, including non-Indian ones. A second goal has been to outline the various historical and geographical origins of the major tales. And finally we shall be looking at the inner meanings of the tales—the psychological origins.

I would like to express my gratitude to all the kind people in four museums across Canada. Many thanks also to Sean Fitzpatrick and Kathryn Scharf, for help with the research; to Daryl Spencer, for the translations from Russian; and to Linda Matthews, for being such a patient and encouraging editor.

Introduction

THE PRINCIPAL MYTHICAL FIGURE OF INDIAN TRIBES ALONG THE northwest coast of North America, and in easternmost Siberia, is called Raven. His form and behavior are based somewhat on the biological raven—*Corvus corax,* the black, raucous, hawk-sized scavenger so conspicuous around settlements in the Pacific Northwest. Prominently featured in artifacts from spoons and bowls to gigantic ceremonial totem poles, Raven is the protagonist in a cycle of folktales told among the Tlingit, Haida, Tsimshian, Kwakiutl, and other Canadian and Alaskan tribes, and among the Siberian Koryak and Chukchi.

But a raven figure appears in the myths of other cultures as well. In Western tradition, the raven is associated with the Greco-Roman god Apollo and the Norse god Odin. The Ainu of Japan, the Australian aborigines, the Malays, and the Vietnamese have stories of a raven or crow that are often tantalizingly similar to those of the Raven figure of Siberia and North America.

One important tale is actually the familiar Noah's-ark story, often referred to as "The Deluge," which spread throughout North American Indian culture long ago. It somewhat resembles "The Earth Diver," a popular Siberian and North American myth about an animal that created dry land (i.e., the earth as we know it) by diving down into the primordial water to bring back some mud.

When we read a North American tale of a great flood, it is usually a combination of these two original stories.

In the case of "The Deluge" and "The Earth Diver," there is indisputable evidence that the North American tales have Old World origins. When, on the other hand, we read of how Raven pretended to be a great chief and went travelling with the slave who acted as his "speaker," we may be sure we are dealing with a tale invented on the Northwest Coast. In the case of other stories, such as the one explaining that the raven was originally turned black by fire, one can only speculate whether the tale was invented by one culture and transmitted to others, or whether the tale arose independently in several different cultures.

In the following text, the Northwest Coast Tlingit tales are presented first and in the most detail. Then the stories are traced eastward to Hudson Bay, southward into the United States, and westward into Asia. In each culture, Raven can play one or more roles: trickster, transformer, culture hero, creator.

The stories presented in these pages often appear in rather abbreviated forms. When they were originally being told, they would have been considerably embellished. When people were sitting around the fire, trying to while away the long hours of a blustery winter night, the storyteller would undoubtedly stretch out any one of the Raven tales considerably, with each subplot contrived to get a laugh or gasp from the audience.

Furthermore, the Raven tales have been recorded in many versions, because the tales are essentially oral; they have been passed on by word of mouth, from generation to generation, and they are usually centuries old, and very widespread.

The Raven tales are *folktales*, "traditional prose tales," to use Stith Thompson's definition. The storyteller does not try to be original; on the contrary, a good storyteller is one who can remember a story in detail, who can tell it without deviating from its traditional form. Nevertheless, each person who tells a particular story is bound to tell it in a slightly different way, and one part of the world may have a general form of that story which differs from the general form in another part of the world.

Over the last hundred years or so, the Raven tales have been put in writing, so they are no longer purely oral, and a number of partial studies of the tales have been done.

As the photographs accompanying this text indicate, Raven is as important a figure in Northwest Coast art as he is in its literature. In looking at these photographs, please keep the following five points in mind:

(1) Northwest Coast art is largely *applied* art; it is used to decorate utilitarian objects.

(2) The designs usually represent animals, among them, of course, Raven.

(3) The two-dimensional art tends to be more abstract than the three-dimensional.

(4) The art is often symmetrical, and abstract two-dimensional artwork frequently shows the animal split in two, spreading to the left and right.

(5) Two-dimensional artwork generally contains very little blank space: an "eye" figure is often used as a filler, or to represent the joints of the animal's body, and the animal's inner anatomy may be displayed in X-ray fashion.

There are some major exceptions to these rules: for example, masks and totem poles are not utilitarian objects, and the art of the Kwakiutl and Salish tends to be less of the applied sort and also less abstract.

Raven is fairly easy to spot in Northwest Coast art. He has a long heavy beak with only a slight curve to the tip, whereas hawks, eagles, and some other birds have a pronounced fish-hook tip to their beaks. Other mythical birds that one could confuse with Raven can be distinguished by the goat-like horns on top of their heads. Most importantly, Raven is usually depicted with the sun or moon in his mouth. He appears in this manner as the main figure on the "raven rattle"; on the back of the rattle are a man, a kingfisher or crane, and sometimes a frog, all of whom depict the guardian spirit quest (Gould n.d., ii–iii, 32–33).

Another mythical raven appears among the Kwakiutl, as a figure in one of their secret societies (Alexander 1964, 245–49). The mask of this character has a beak several feet long. He and Grizzly Bear are the companions of the Cannibal Spirit, who lives at the north end of the world, and this Raven feeds on the eyes and brains of men whom the Cannibal Spirit has devoured.

Village of Skidegate, Queen Charlotte Islands, British Columbia, 1878 (Haida). *Photograph courtesy of the National Museums of Canada/Canadian Museum of Civilization, 255.*

1

THE
TLINGIT
RAVEN TALES

THE TLINGIT INDIANS LIVE ON THE NORTHWEST coast of North America; their territory extends from southern Alaska to northern British Columbia. The land of the Tlingit is one of high mountains and thick forests, but the Tlingit confine themselves largely to the coast, where fish are abundant, and where the water allows easier travel than the dense forests. The traditional domicile of the Tlingit was the huge multi-family plank house, similar to those used by other cultures of the Northwest Coast. Their economy was based mainly on fishing. They caught salmon, halibut, and other large fish in the sea and in the river mouths. Although their diet was supplemented by roots, berries, and seaweed, the oil from a small fish called the eulachon (also spelled "oolichan") or candlefish made up for the shortage of carbohydrate foods.

In comparison with the inland tribes, the Tlingit (and other coastal tribes) were rich in material goods. Sea-otter furs, native copper, and blankets of mountain-goat wool were traded for slaves and shell ornaments from the south. When white men began buying furs from the Tlingit, their wealth was increased by white men's products. One's wealth was displayed at the potlatch, a feast at which valuable property was given away, increasing the prestige of the giver and his family.

Tlingit social structure was complex. Each person was born into either the Raven or the Wolf moiety, but he also belonged to a clan, members of which could trace their relationship to a common ancestor, as well as to an even smaller social division, the lineage group. The Tlingit were matrilineal: one's ancestry was traced along the female line, not the male. They were also exogamous, i.e., one had to marry outside one's own moiety. In early times, a village usually consisted of a single lineage group, and each village was politically independent.

Again like other coastal peoples, the Tlingit had a strong concept of status. From slave to chief, each person knew his place in society.

Tlingit wealth allowed an indulgence in art. Visual art included carving, particularly in cedar wood, and among the carved objects were house posts and so-called totem poles, which actually represented the heraldic crests of the owners or served to depict myths, but bowls, rattles, and other objects also illustrate Tlingit carving.

One of the most conspicuous animals in Tlingit territory is the raven, *Corvus corax*, one of the largest members of the crow family; the bird is omnivorous but lives to a large extent on carrion. It is this creature who plays the leading role in Tlingit stories. The Raven stories are many, and they take many forms. Raven may be a "trickster," a foolish creature who deceives, lies, and steals, to satisfy his greed—but who often becomes the victim of his own duplicity. On the other hand, Raven may also be a "transformer," one who arranges the land, sea, and sky, and the animals living on earth, to give them their present structures; it was Raven, for example, who is said to have put the sun in the sky. He is also a "culture hero," one who gives mankind the things it needs to survive, particularly fire, or who teaches humans how to take care of themselves. To some extent, the Tlingit and their neighbors regard Raven as a "creator," the deity who was responsible for the very existence of the world, or at least its present form. But for the sake of simplicity, I shall be placing the tales in only two categories: origin tales and trickster tales.

Raven, in fact, is the principal mythical figure of the Northwest Coast of North America and of easternmost Siberia. The Raven tales are found primarily among the Tlingit, Haida, and Tsimshian of the Northwest Coast, but the same tales are found to a varying extent among most of the other tribes of Alaska, the Yukon, and western British Columbia. The western Eskimo and the Aleut have tales closely resembling those of the Tlingit. So do many of the northern Athapaskan tribes, spread over much of northwestern North America: the Tahltan, Eyak, Chilcotin, Tanana, Tanaina, Kutchin, Chipewyan, and so on. Further south, an important group is the speakers of Wakashan languages: the Nootka, Kwakiutl, Heiltsuk, and Oweekeno. The tales occasionally appear among the Salish Indians, such as the Halkomelem, Bella Coola, Comox, Lillooet, and Shuswap. South of British Columbia the tales extend intermittently from the Quileute of northern Washington to the Yurok of northern California. The Chukchi and Koryak of Siberia have a Raven cycle that closely parallels that of the Tlingit and Haida both in completeness and in the content of individual tales. Finally, what might be called "borderline" Raven tales can be found all over North America and Siberia.

The Tlingit variants are a good starting point for a study of the tales, for several reasons. In the first place, the Tlingit refer to Raven by a local word, Yetl, which actually means "raven." The Haida name is Nankilslas, meaning "He Whose Voice Is Obeyed," the Tsimshian name is Txamsem, meaning "Giant," and the various Kwakiutl groups use names meaning "Real Chief" (Hemaskas), "Great Inventor" (Kwekwaxawe), "Greedy One" (Meskwa), or "Chief" (Omeatl) (Boas [1916] 1970, 584). Generally he is regarded as related to the biological raven, but among the Tsimshian (Boas [1916] 1970, 60) and Kwakiutl (Boas 1895, 175) he is only raven-like in the sense that he has a "raven cloak," with which he can fly. These names that do not mean "raven" may be nicknames or terms of respect, but their use suggests, although it does not prove, that the Raven tales have been grafted onto those of a prior, more anthropomorphic character.

Secondly, of the forty-five principal Raven tales listed by Boas ([1916] 1970, 583-84), thirty-seven are found among the Tlingit, whereas for the Tsimshian there are only thirty-two, and for the

Kwakiutl there are only thirty-three. There are thirty-nine Haida tales (ignoring a typographic error in Boas' list), but they tend to be less developed than the Tlingit ones. The Haida stories are also a little atypical: "The Theft of the Sun" becomes "The Theft of the Moon" and loses its usual ending; in fact, the entire story seems to lose its place as the first event in the series of Raven's transformations, and another transformation is substituted, in which Raven creates the Haida country and the mainland from two pebbles (Gould n.d., 146–48).

Finally, the Tlingit are the northernmost of the tribes possessing a fully developed Raven cycle, and as such their tales may form a link with those of eastern Siberia.

ORIGIN TALES

1 The Birth of Raven; The Deluge

In the Tlingit story of Raven's birth, there are two "Raven" characters, Raven-at-the-head-of-the-Nass and Raven himself. The story includes references to the relationship between nephew and uncle: because the Tlingit are matrilineal, a boy's maternal uncle is, in many respects, a more important figure than his father. When a man dies, his nephew (sister's son) inherits the wives, social prerogatives, and material wealth of the deceased.

> . . . There lived in a house at the head of the Nass river a being called Raven-at-the-head-of-Nass (Nas-caki-yel). . . .
>
> First of all beings Nas-caki-yel created the Heron (Laq) as a very tall and very wise man and after him the Raven (Yel), who was also a very good and very wise man at that time.
>
> Raven came into being in this wise. His first mother had many children, but they all died young, and she cried over them continually. According to some, this woman was Nas-caki-yel's sister and it was Nas-caki-yel who was doing this because he did not wish her to have any male children. By and by Heron came to her and said, "What is that you are crying about all the time?" She answered, "I am always

losing my children. I can not bring them up." Then he said, "Go down on the beach when the tide is lowest, get a small, smooth stone, and put it into the fire. When it is red hot, swallow it. Do not be afraid." She said, "All right." Then she followed Heron's directions and gave birth to Raven. Therefore Raven's name was really Itcaku, the name of a very hard rock, and he was hence called Taqlik-ic (Hammer-father). This is why Raven was so tough and could not easily be killed. (Swanton 1909, 81–82)

An incident usually recounted here, but omitted from this version, is that Raven goes to the house of his uncle Raven-at-the-head-of-the-Nass and seduces his aunt, of whom the uncle is so jealous that he keeps her locked up in a box. But the rivalry has already been established without that further provocation. The story continues:

. . . [Raven] shot a bird called cax [loon (Boas [1916] 1970, 621)] and a large bird which was very pretty and had a bill that looked like copper. . . . Then Nas-caki-yel said, "Go and fell that tree standing over there," for he wanted the tree to kill him. But when the tree fell upon Raven it could not kill him because he was made of rock. Finding him still alive, Nas-caki-yel called him in the following day and said, "Go and clean out that canoe." It was a canoe just being made [i.e., a dugout, with spreaders inserted to widen it], and when Raven got into it to clean it, it closed upon him. Then he simply extended his elbows and broke the canoe after which he smashed it up for firewood. All this Nas-caki-yel saw, and again sent for him. He came in, and they put into the fire a large copper kettle made like a box, filled it with water, and put heated stones into it. Then they [i.e., Nas-caki-yel's servants] told him to get in, and they covered it over in order to kill him. Raven, however, again changed himself into a rock, and, when they thought he was cooked to pieces and looked inside, they saw that he was still there. Then they told him to come out.

Now Nas-caki-yel was very angry and said, "Let rain pour down all over the world, and let people die of starvation." Then it became so wet and stormy that people could not get food and began to starve. Their canoes were also broken up, their homes fell in on them, and they suffered terribly. Now Nas-caki-yel asked for his jointed dance hat and when he put it on, water began pouring out of the very top of it. When the water rose so as to cover the house floor, Raven and his mother got upon the lowest retaining timber. This house we are talking of, although it looked like a house to them, was really part of the world. It had eight rows of retaining timbers, and, as the water came up, Raven and his mother climbed to a higher one. At the same time the people of the world were climbing up into the hills. When the waters reached the fourth retaining timber they were halfway up the mountains. When the house was nearly full of water, Raven had his mother get into the skin of the cax he had killed, while he got into the skin of the white bird with the copper-colored bill, and to this very day Tlingit do not eat the cax because it was Raven's mother. The cax, which is a great diver, now stayed on the surface of the water, but Raven himself flew to the highest cloud in the sky and hung there by his bill.

After Raven had hung to this cloud for days and days, nobody knows how long, he pulled his bill out and prayed to fall upon a piece of kelp, for he thought that the water had gone down. He did so, and, flying off, found the waters just half way down the mountains. (Swanton 1909, 119–20)

2 Raven Becomes Voracious

"Raven never got full because he had eaten the black spots off his own toes. He learned about this after having inquired everywhere for some way of bringing such a state about. Then he wandered through all the world in search of things to eat" (Swanton 1909, 17–18).

3 The Theft of the Sun

. . . There was no light in this world, but it was told him [i.e., Raven] that far up the Nass was a large house in which some one kept light just for himself.

Raven thought over all kinds of plans for getting this light into the world and finally he hit on a good one. The rich man living there had a daughter, and he thought, "I will make myself very small and drop into the water in the form of a small piece of dirt." The girl swallowed this dirt and became pregnant. When her time was completed, they made a hole for her, as was customary, in which she was to bring forth, and lined it with rich furs of all sorts. But the child did not wish to be born on these fine things. Then its grandfather felt sad and said, "What do you think it would be best to put into that hole? Shall we put in moss?" So they put moss inside and the baby was born on it. Its eyes were very bright and moved around rapidly.

Round bundles of varying shapes and sizes hung about on the walls of the house. When the child became a little larger it crawled around back of the people weeping continually, and as it cried it pointed to the bundles. This lasted many days. Then its grandfather said, "Give my grandchild what he is crying for. Give him that one hanging on the end. That is the bag of stars." So the child played with this, rolling it about on the floor back of the people, until suddenly he let it go through the smoke hole. It went straight up into the sky and the stars scattered out of it, arranging themselves as you now see them. That was what he went there for.

Some time after this he began crying again, and he cried so much that it was thought he would die. Then his grandfather said, "Untie the next one and give it to him." He played and played with it around behind his mother. After a while he let that go up through the smoke hole also, and there was the big moon.

Now just one more thing remained, the box that held the daylight, and he cried for that. His eyes turned around and showed different colors, and the people began thinking that he must be something other than an ordinary baby. But it always happens that a grandfather loves his grandchild just as he does his own daughter, so the grandfather said, "Untie the last thing and give it to him." His grandfather felt very sad when he gave this to him. When the child had this in his hands, he uttered the raven cry, "Ga," and flew out with it through the smoke hole. Then the person from whom he had stolen it said, "That old manuring raven has gotten all of my things." (Swanton 1909, 3–4)

In another version recorded by Swanton (1909, 81–82), the owner of the sun is Nas-caki-yel, who elsewhere appears as Raven's uncle. The identification of the sun-owner with Raven's uncle is a neat tying-together of part of the plot, and a response to the otherwise unanswered question of the sun-owner's name, but it is not supported by other Northwest Coast versions of "The Theft of the Sun."

The narrator then tries to tie the story together by adding: "Because Nas-caki-yel got it into his mind to wish for daylight in the world, he had wished for a grandchild through whom it might come" (Swanton 1909, 82). Yet it is illogical for Nas-caki-yel to want daylight for the world, and for Raven to then trick him into giving it up.

4 Raven Threatens to Let Out the Light

> Then Raven, who was already quite large, walked down along the bank of Nass river until he heard the noise people were making as they fished along the shore for eulachon in the darkness. All the people in the world then lived at one place at the mouth of the Nass. They had already heard that Nas-caki-yel had something called "daylight," which would some day come into the world, and they used to talk about it a great deal. They were afraid of it.
>
> Then Raven shouted to the fishermen, "Why do you make so much noise? If you make so much noise I will break daylight on you." Eight canoe loads of people were fishing there. But they answered, "You are not Nas-caki-yel. How can you have the daylight?", and the noise continued. Then Raven opened the box a little and light shot over the world like lightning. At that they made still more noise. So he opened the box completely and there was daylight everywhere.
>
> When this daylight burst upon the people they were very much frightened, and some ran into the water, some into the woods. Those that had hair-seal or fur-seal skins for clothing ran into the water and became hair seals and fur seals. Hair seal and fur seal were formerly only the names of the clothing they had. Those who had skins called marten skins, black-bear skins, grizzly-bear skins, etc., ran into the woods and turned into such animals. (Swanton 1909, 8–283)

Another version is almost identical except that Raven sees people catching eulachon on the far bank of a river. He asks to be taken across and they refuse, even when he threatens to let out the daylight. They are thrown down when he opens the box a little, and when they still refuse he lets the sun out completely, and they are transformed into the various animals (Swanton 1909, 5).

In a third Tlingit version, Raven asks the fishermen to give him some fish in return for daylight. They call him a liar, telling him that he cannot make daylight, and refuse to give him any fish. He lifts one wing and lets the moon shine out, so they believe him and give him some herring. But he is still angry, so he takes some pine needles and puts them into the herrings, so that herrings are now full of little bones. Then he puts the sun, moon, and stars in the sky. When it becomes day, the people run away, turning into various kinds of fish, birds and mammals. That is how the animals were created (Boas 1895, 313).

5 The Theft of Fresh Water

Journeying on, Raven was told of another place, where a man had an everlasting spring of water. This man was named Petrel (Ganuk). Raven wanted this water because there was none to drink in this world, but Petrel always slept by this spring, and he had a cover over it so as to keep it all to himself. Then Raven came in and said to him, "My brother-in-law, I have just come to see you. How are you?" He told Petrel of all kinds of things that were happening outside, trying to induce him to go out to look at them, but Petrel was too smart for him and refused.

When night came, Raven said, "I am going to sleep with you, brother-in-law." So they went to bed, and toward morning Raven heard Petrel sleeping very soundly. Then he went outside, took some dog manure and put it around Petrel's buttocks. When it was beginning to grow light, he said, "Wake up, wake up, wake up, brother-in-law, you have defecated all over your clothes." Petrel got up, looked at himself, and thought it was true, so he took his blankets and went outside. Then Raven went over to Petrel's spring, took off the cover and began drinking. After he had drunk up almost all of the water, Petrel came in and saw him. Then Raven flew straight up, crying, "Ga."

Before he got through the smoke hole, however, Petrel said, "My spirits up the smoke hole, catch him." So Raven stuck there, and Petrel put pitchwood on the fire under him so as to make a quantity of smoke. Raven was white before that time, but the smoke made him of the color you find him to-day. Still he did not drop the water. When the smoke-hole spirits let him go, he flew around the nearest point and rubbed himself all over so as to clear off as much of the soot as possible.

This happened somewhere about the Nass, and afterwards he started up this way. First he let some water fall from his mouth and made the Nass. By and by he spit more out and made the Stikine. Next he spit out the Taku river, then Chilkat, then Alsek, and all the other large rivers. The small drops that came out of his mouth made the small salmon creeks. (Swanton 1909, 4)

In another version, when Raven has stolen the water, he perches in a tree, and Petrel lights a fire under the tree, blackening Raven with the smoke (Krause [1885] 1956, 178).

6 The Origin of Eulachon

Raven starts an argument with Gull, who then flies out to sea and returns with an eulachon. Gull will not give the fish to Raven, but swallows it himself. Raven sees Heron (or Crane) and tells him that Gull is calling him names. He tells Heron to go and kick Gull in the stomach. Heron does so, and Gull then vomits up the eulachon, which Raven swallows (Swanton 1909, 13–14; Krause [1885] 1956, 180–81). There is actually more to the story, but not in the Tlingit versions.

7 The Origin of the Tides

Raven comes to a door in a cliff. He knows that the old woman in charge of the tides lives there. He begins eating sea urchins, and she says, "On what low tide did you get those?" He tells her to be quiet, but she will not, so he sticks sea-urchin spines into her buttocks. He only stops when she promises to let the tides rise and fall regularly. (Swanton 1909, 9–10, 120).

8 War with the South Wind

The tale of "War with the South Wind" is the story of how Raven obtained good weather. It is found among the Tsimshian, Haida, Nootka, and Kwakiutl, but apparently not among the Tlingit.

9 The Theft of Fire

Leaving this place, Raven came to another where he saw something floating not far from shore, though it never came any nearer. He assembled all kinds of fowl. Toward evening he looked at the object and saw that it resembled fire. So he told a chicken hawk (kaku) which had a very long bill to fly out to it, saying, "Be very brave. If you get some of that fire, do not let go of it." The chicken hawk reached the place, seized some fire and started back as fast as it could fly, but by the time it got the fire to Raven its bill was burned off. That is why its bill is short. Then Raven took some red cedar, and some white stones called *neq* which are found on the beach, and he put fire into them so that it could be found ever afterward all over the world. (Swanton 1909, 11)

In another Tlingit version, it is Raven himself who carries off the fire, burning his beak in the process (Boas [1916] 1970, 661–62).

10 The Origin of Humans; The Origin of Death

Swanton records two versions of a story that accounts for both the origin of humans and the origin of death.

After all the human beings had been destroyed Raven made new ones out of leaves. Because he made this new generation, people know that he must have changed all of the first people who had survived the flood, into stones. Since human beings were made from leaves people always die off rapidly in the fall of the year when flowers and leaves are falling off. (Swanton 1909, 18)

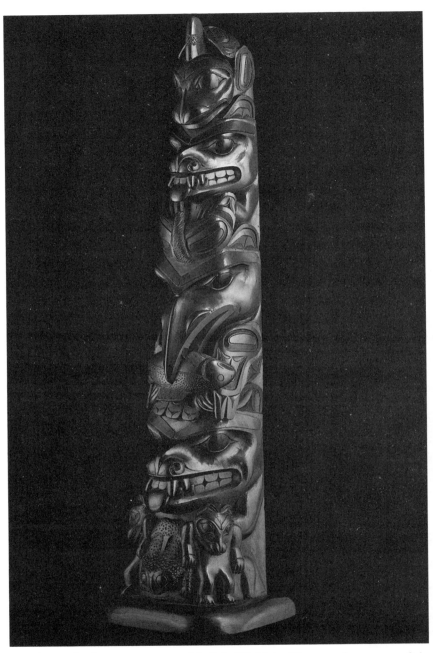

Argillite pole depicting raven with fish (Haida). *Photograph courtesy of the Royal British Columbia Museum, Victoria, British Columbia, CPN 4786.*

In the second version, the creation of humans is ascribed to Raven's uncle:

Nas-caki-yel tried to make human beings out of a rock and out of a leaf at the same time, but the rock was slow while the leaf was very quick. Therefore human beings came from the leaf. Then he showed a leaf to the human beings and said, "You see this leaf. You are to be like it. When it falls off the branch and rots there is nothing left of it." That is why there is death in the world. If men had come from the rock there would be no death. Years ago people used to say when they were getting old, "We are unfortunate in not having been made from a rock. Being made from a leaf, we must die." (Swanton 1909, 81)

Boas has a more elaborate version:

Yetl [Raven] wanted to create humans. He created human forms out of stone. He breathed on them, and the stones became alive, but they soon died again. Then he made human shapes out of earth and breathed on them, and they became alive. But they also died again soon. He carved humans from wood and gave them life by breathing on them. They also soon died. Then he made human shapes out of grass and breathed on them. They came to life and became the ancestors of mankind. For that reason, humans grow up and die like grass. (1895, 319)

11 The Painting of the Birds

The Tlingit have no tale that actually describes the birds painting each other. They have one story, however, which elsewhere forms part of "The Painting of the Birds." In the Tlingit story, the birds decorate each other, and Blue Jay, for example, has his hair tied up with a string, so that blue jays (i.e., Steller's jays) now have crests (Swanton 1909, 6). We shall be looking at "The Painting of the Birds" in more detail in later chapters.

12 The Origin of Fog

Raven paddles his canoe until he meets Petrel, who is in another canoe. They argue about who is older. Petrel pushes Raven's canoe away and puts on his "fog hat," creating a fog, so that Raven cannot see where he is going. Raven admits that Petrel must be older than he, and tells him to "let that hat go into the world." So now we know that if a fog arrives in a clearing and then goes back again, it will be good weather (Swanton 1909, 10–11).

13 The Origin of Salmon

Raven marries the daughter of Fog-over-the-salmon. Raven is hungry, so his wife washes her hands in a basket, and a salmon appears in the basket. She continues to produce salmon in this way, and they dry a lot of it. One day, Raven and his wife quarrel, and he hits her with a piece of salmon. She runs away, and when he tries to grab her, his hands pass through her body, because she is fog. He goes to his father-in-law and begs him to get the woman back, but his father-in-law says that Raven has broken his promise to respect the woman, and so he cannot have her back (Swanton 1909, 108).

TRICKSTER TALES

14 Raven Kills the Salmon

Raven and his nephews the crows are down at the beach one day. Raven tempts a salmon to come close to shore and then kills it. He sends his nephews to fetch skunk-cabbage leaves to wrap the salmon for steaming. When they have gone, he eats the fish. The crows return, and Raven pretends to be asleep. He opens his eyes, accuses the crows of the theft, and throws ashes on them to blacken their previously white plumage (Swanton 1909, 5–6; Krause [1885] 1956, 181–82).

15 The Killing of Grizzly Bear

Raven invites Grizzly Bear to go fishing with him. Raven catches plenty of fish, and Grizzly Bear asks Raven what he is using for bait. Raven replies that he is using his testicles. Grizzly Bear cuts off his own testicles and dies (Swanton 1909, 6–7; Krause [1885] 1956, 182). (Then follows the incident of Raven's tearing out Cormorant's tongue; see below.)

Raven then feeds Grizzly Bear's wife with halibut stomachs filled with hot rocks, after which he gives her water to drink. The water turns to steam, and she is killed (Swanton 1909, 7–8; Krause [1885] 1956, 182).

16 Cormorant's Tongue Is Torn Out

Cormorant has accompanied Raven on the fishing trip with Grizzly Bear, and Raven wants Cormorant to keep quiet about the killing. He says that there is a louse on the side of Cormorant's head. He pretends to pick it off and then tells Cormorant to open his mouth so that Raven can feed it to him. When Cormorant opens his mouth, Raven tears out his tongue, so now cormorants only make a gabbling sound (Boas [1916] 1970, 678–80).

17 The Killing of Pitch

Pitch has a house full of halibut, and Raven asks him where he has caught them. Pitch reluctantly goes with Raven to show him, but it is a hot, sunny day, so he melts away and dies. Then Raven goes to Pitch's house and eats his fill of Pitch's halibut (Krause [1885] 1956, 182).

18 Raven's Beak Is Torn Off

Some people are fishing, and Raven goes under the water and tries to steal the bait from their hooks, but his beak gets caught on a hook. They try to pull him in, but he braces himself against the bottom of the canoe until his beak is pulled off. They think it is the nose of a monster and hang it on a wall. Raven makes himself a fake nose out of spruce gum, pulls a hat down over his face, and enters the house, asking to see the monster's nose. When he sees it, he grabs it, puts it back on his face, and flies out through the smoke hole (Swanton 1909, 8, 84–85).

19 Raven Is Swallowed by a Whale

Raven sees a whale out at sea, and he takes a knife and some fire-making equipment and flies into the whale's mouth. When the whale opens its mouth again, fish pour in. Raven lives off the fish for a while, then decides to eat the fat from the whale. Finally he decides to cut out the whale's heart and eat it, and the whale dies. Raven uses magic to make the whale drift to shore. He calls until people hear him and cut the whale open, releasing him. Raven quickly flies off and waits until the people have finished rendering the whale's fat into oil. He asks them if they heard a noise when they first saw the whale. They say they had, and that something flew away when they cut the whale open. Raven tells them that the last time an event like that had occurred, the people involved had been killed. So everyone hearing Raven's story runs away, and he has all the oil to himself (Swanton 1909, 12–13, 91–92).

20 Raven Travels with His Slave

The story of Raven and his slave forms an unusually cohesive series of events. Part of the story involves the fact that a chief must not address his underlings directly, but only through an intermediary, a "speaker."

Yetl [Raven] went on and found a raspberry bush. He shook it and changed it into a man, whom he named Kitsino, and told him that he must serve him as a speaker. They went on together and soon came to a village, in which large amounts of supplies were stored. The chief of the village invited Yetl to a meal and asked him what he would like.

Yetl said to Kitsino, "Say that I would like fish." But Kitsino said: "The great chief wants nothing to eat." "Oh, don't say that!" said Yetl, "say that I would like to eat fish." But again spoke Kitsino: "The great chief wants nothing to eat." So it happened that the raven remained hungry, while all the others ate and drank.

They went on and came to a village in which there were great supplies of fish oil. Yetl spoke to Kitsino: "We will go into the house of the chiefs. There some oil will get into my eye. Then say to the people that I will soon die. When I am dead, place me in a box and tell all the people to go away. But don't let them take any fish oil with them." The chief of the village entertained Yetl and Kitsino, and in the evening everyone lay down and slept. But in the night some fish oil squirted into Yetl's eye and he became sick. He rubbed his eye all day and finally he died. Then Kitsino sang songs of mourning without end. He laid him in a small box and said to the people: "Now tie the box up tightly. I know he is only pretending to be dead." They obeyed and hung the box up on the roof beam. Now Kitsino commanded the people to go away and forbade then to take fish oil with them. He said to them that if they did not obey, sickness and misfortune would visit them. The people went away and Yetl and Kitsino remained behind by themselves. Raven wanted to come out of the box, but found himself tightly bound. Kitsino began to eat what he found, and sampled everything. Yetl heard him eating and jumped around in the box. He cried: "Don't eat it all up! Don't eat it all up!" He moved around so violently that the box finally fell on the floor, rolled around and broke. Meanwhile Kitsino had eaten all the oil and there was only some dried meat left over for Yetl.

The final section of the story sees the end of the slave. In the following version, he is called Butterfly.

Yetl began a friendship with Butterfly, and together they wandered all over the world. At one time they came to a long fjord. They wanted to go across it, and after a long search Yetl found a piece of giant kelp, which he stretched across for a bridge. But when he crossed over the fjord, Butterfly was afraid to follow. Raven, who soon reached the opposite side, called to him to cross over in the same way he himself had done. But Butterfly cried: "No, I'll fall into the water." When

Butterfly finally stepped onto the bridge of kelp, Raven made it revolve. Then Butterfly drowned and his corpse drifted to land. Yetl went down to the shore, cut him up and ate his intestines. Then he buried him under a stone. After a while he returned to the grave, revived Butterfly, and said: "Oh, friend, I thought you were lost. I looked for you for so long, and now here you are sleeping." (Boas 1895, 314–15)

21 Raven Gathers Poor Food

Then Raven went about picking up the smallest fish, as bull heads and tom cod, which he strung on a stick, while a friend who was with him at this time, named Cakaku, took large creatures like whales. With the grease he boiled out, Cakaku filled an entire house, while Raven filled only a small bladder.

Raven stayed with Cakaku and one night had a dream. He said to his friend, "I dreamed that a great enemy came and attacked us." Then he had all the fowls assemble and come to fight, so that his dream might be fulfilled. As soon as Raven had told his dream, Cakaku went down and saw the birds. Then Raven went into the house and began drinking up his grease. But the man came back, saw what Raven was doing, and threw him into a grease box, which he started to tie up with a strong rope. Raven, however, called out, "My brother, do not tie me up with a strong rope, but take a straw such as our forefathers used to employ." He did so. Then Raven drank up all the grease in the box, and, when the man took him up on a high cliff and kicked him off, he came out easily and flew away crying "Ga." (Swanton 1909, 17)

22 Raven Becomes a Woman

Raven decides to turn into a woman. Some killer whales come by, paddling a canoe, and Raven marries one of them. When Raven reaches their village, people think she is important, because only the daughter of a chief is ever fetched by canoe.

The whales' food supply starts to disappear mysteriously: the grease in the boxes is dwindling. Raven has a labret, set with abalone shell, and one day it is found in one of the boxes of grease. Raven tells the whales that the labret has the bad habit of wandering off wherever it wants to go.

Raven claims one day that she has had a dream that her husband has died. That night she sharpens a stick and uses it to kill her husband. The next morning the other whales hear her mourning his death.

She tells the whales to leave her far from town, with her husband's body. No one dares to go near her, but she is actually eating the whale's body.

Later she sees various kinds of white birds flying overhead, and she claims that she had made them white. The whales ask her to make them white, too. She tells them that she can do so, but that it will hurt and they will have to be brave. She has them all lie down in a row, and she pokes her sharpened stick into their ears, killing all but the last whale, who leaps into the sea, crying "Raven has finished us sure enough" (Swanton 1909, 114–16).

23 The Bungling Host

The next story is very popular throughout North America, although it is only on the Northwest Coast that one of the characters is Raven. In the following version, Bear has invited Raven to a meal.

> Then Bear told him to sit down and said, "I will roast some dry salmon for you." So he began to roast it. After it was done, he set a dish close to the fire and slit the back of his hands with a knife so as to let grease run out for Raven to eat on his salmon. After he had fixed the salmon, he cut a piece of flesh out from in front of his thighs and put it into the dish. That is why bears are not fat in that place.
>
> Now Raven wanted to give a dinner to Bear in return, so he, too, took out a piece of fish, roasted it, set out the dish Bear had used, close to the fire and slit up the back of his hand, thinking that grease would run out of it. But instead nothing but white bubbles came forth. Although he knew he could not do it, he tried in every way. (Swanton 1909, 6)

24 The Visit to Shadow Town

Then [Raven] went up a river in his boat, until he found a house. He went inside, but saw no people. The house was inhabited by shadows and feathers, that floated to and fro in there. At first Raven was frightened, but then he saw lots of halibut and fat from deer and mountain goats stored up there in boxes, so he decided to go in and cook himself a dish of halibut with mountain-goat fat. When the meal was cooked, he looked for a bowl, but he couldn't find one. Then one of the shadows brought him a bowl, and Yetl was glad that he had found such good hosts. He ate until he couldn't eat any more, then put the rest in his basket and went down to the boat. He intended to leave, when it occurred to him that it would be a great pity to leave behind all those good foodstuffs in the boxes. He turned around and collected all the provisions of the shadows and feathers. But then they immediately attacked him, beat him until he could no longer move, and threw him out of the house. When he finally pulled himself together and hobbled down to his boat, he found it completely empty. He was sad, he went back home and put himself to bed. His face and back were swollen from the blows he had received. When someone asked him what had struck him, he said that he had fallen off a rock. (Boas 1895, 316–17)

25 Raven Kills Deer

Raven pretends to be friends with Deer. He makes a bridge of wild celery (cow parsnip) stalks or a rotten stick and runs across without breaking it, because he is light. He tells Deer to cross also, but Deer is reluctant. Finally he does attempt to cross, but the bridge breaks, and Deer plunges to his death. Raven eats the body, and when the other animals arrive and ask Raven where his friend Deer is, Raven says that wild animals have devoured him, and he pretends to be in mourning (Swanton 1909, 8–9, 107).

Most of the better-known Raven tales are found among the Tlingit, but there are a few major stories that are missing from the Tlingit Raven cycle. We shall be looking at these in the next chapter.

Besides "War with the South Wind," they are:

26 Raven Steals Salmon Eggs
27 Raven Steals His Sisters' Berries
28 Raven Burns a Girl's Groins
29 The Master Fisherman
30 War with the Thunderbird
31 The Arrow of the Supernatural Being

Raven rattle. *Photograph courtesy of the Royal Ontario Museum, Toronto, HN401.*

2

RAVEN TALES ELSEWHERE IN NORTH AMERICA

THROUGHOUT MOST OF BRITISH COLUMBIA, Alaska, and the Yukon, the Raven tales of other tribes are similar to those of the Tlingit. The tales of the basic Raven cycle appear sporadically further east and south of these areas. Yet the main elements of the stories are sometimes found again very far from the Northwest Coast, for example among the Shoshone and Jicarilla Apache of the plains.

ORIGIN TALES

1 The Birth of Raven; The Deluge

The story of Raven's birth has two principal motifs, "The Jealous Uncle," and "The Earth Diver" or "The Deluge." "The Earth Diver" is set at the beginning of the world; water covers everything, and animals are sent down to bring back a piece of earth, from which the creator can form dry land. "The Deluge," on the other hand, is not set at the beginning of the world: the water has been sent as punishment by the creator, and the main characters save themselves in a boat. The story of Noah's ark, in the Bible, is a good example of the deluge story. "The Earth Diver" or "The Deluge," or—more often—

a combination of the two, is found in every part of North America, except among some of the Eskimo. The raven or crow can play any of a number of characters.

"The Birth of Raven," with its accompanying deluge or earth diver tale, has three general forms: Tlingit, Haida, and Tsimshian-Kwakiutl (Boas [1916] 1970, 621–41). Versions found among the Tahltan, Eyak, and Aleut are similar to those of the Tlingit (Teit 1919, 199–200; Birket-Smith and De Laguna 1938, 257–58; Liapunova 1987, 8–9). Beyond the Northwest Coast area itself, a change occurs: instead of being joined to "The Birth of Raven," "The Deluge" and/or "The Earth Diver" appears as an independent story—or two.

Haida

The Haida versions are highly variable, and the story actually begins shortly after the birth of Raven, but the basic form is as follows.

Chief Hole-in-His-Fin (Killer Whale) and his wife Flood-Tide Woman have a son, Raven, who will not stop crying until his father's sister Ice Woman takes him in her arms. Raven uses magic to put everyone to sleep, and then he has sexual intercourse with his aunt. At the same time, the chief's nephew has intercourse with the chief's wife. The chief finds out what has happened, and so he sends both his wife Flood-Tide Woman and their son away to live with her brother Great Breakers (or Cape Ball, or Nankilslas).

Raven behaves just as badly in his new home. He constantly bangs the door, he excretes profusely, and when his father and uncle take the form of killer whales in order to catch whales, he causes them to be stranded on the beach.

He shoots birds and saves their skins. When he puts on the skin of a duck, he can swim. When he puts on the skin of a raven, he can fly like a raven. One day his uncle is out hunting seals, and Raven gives his aunt (not to be confused with the first aunt) a love potion in the form of chewing gum, and so he is able to seduce her. It begins to thunder, and his uncle thereby realizes what has happened. He puts on his hat. A whirlpool rushes out of it, and water begins to cover the earth. Raven puts on his raven skin and flies up to the sky. He starts kicking the water, and it finally recedes (Boas [1916] 1970, 625–33).

In several Haida accounts, this deluge story is preceded by one that explains the creation of the Queen Charlotte islands:

> Over this island [i.e., the entire Queen Charlotte group] salt water extended, they say. Raven flew about. He looked for a place upon which to sit. After awhile he flew away to sit upon a flat rock which lay toward the south end of the island. All the supernatural creatures lay upon it . . . with their necks laid across one another. The feebler supernatural beings were stretched out from it in this, that, and every other direction, asleep. It was light then, and yet dark, they say.

Raven flies up into the sky, runs his beak into it, and draws himself up. He discovers a large town. The chief's daughter has just given birth, so Raven skins the child and puts on the skin. One night he gets up and starts removing people's eyes. He roasts the eyes in the fire and eats them. He does the same the next evening, but he is spotted by an old woman, "the Half-rock one," who tells the chief. He is dropped into the water, and he floats around for a while, until a grebe calls to him. He finds himself floating against some kelp, and then discovers a house pole, which he climbs down to discover another world. There he meets an old man, who has a set of five boxes nesting inside one another. The man takes from the innermost box two cylindrical pebbles, one black, the other covered with spots. He tells Raven to put the spotted pebble in the water, then to put the black pebble in the water, and finally to bite off a part of each and spit it upon the rest. Raven does things in the wrong order, but when he does everything properly, the pieces bitten off stick to the main parts to form trees. The black pebble becomes the Haida country (the Queen Charlotte Islands), and the spotted pebble becomes the mainland (Swanton 1905, 110–12).

Raven later travels north, where he finds the family of Chief Hole-in-His-Fin. He enters the skin of the chief's son, and the story continues as before.

In this version, as we have just seen, in place of Raven's birth we find him (twice) entering the body of a baby that has just been born. As Boas points out ([1916] 1970, 629), this means the story is no longer a general introduction to the Raven cycle, but simply an early part of his wanderings. Gould (n.d., 146–48) also sees this Haida story as part of Raven's wanderings rather than as a birth story; she regards it as replacing "The Theft of the Sun" as the first major event in Raven's travels.

Tsimshian and Kwakiutl

The Tsimshian-Kwakiutl versions show even greater variation, but the following may present the general idea.

A chieftainess takes the chief's nephew for her lover. In order to meet him more easily, she pretends to be dead. She is placed in a box in a tree, and the nephew visits her at night. She becomes pregnant and gives birth to a boy. A slave discovers what is happening and tells the chief, who kills his wife but leaves the child in the box. The child lives by sucking his mother's intestines. One day the naked boy, shining like fire, appears from the box and is brought to the chief, who names him Sucking Intestines. The boy grows up. He and a companion dress in bird skins and fly to the "hole of heaven," where the boy marries the daughter of the chief above (or chief of the sun). The boy is subjected to dangerous tricks by the chief. The daughter gives birth to a boy who falls into the sea. The boy is found and adopted (Boas [1916] 1970, 58–60, 634–35).

Kutchin

In the days when the earth was all covered with water, the animals lived on a large raft. The Crow said, "Had I any earth, even so little, I would make it grow large enough for all the animals to live upon." Muskrat, Otter, and many other divers went down under the waters and tried to bring up some earth; but they were all drowned. Last of all, Beaver dived with a line attached to his body. He went so deep that he was almost drowned when he reached the bottom. In his death-struggle he clutched some mud in his paws, and the mud was still there when he was drawn up lifeless by the line. Taking it and running his walking-stick through it, the Crow planted the stick in the water in such a way that the bit of earth rested at the surface of the water. The earth grew larger and larger. When it was big enough to hold all the animals, they stepped onto it from the raft.

The Crow's walking-stick is still supporting the land; and, as it has never rotted, it is still to be seen somewhere about the junction of the Old Crow and the Porcupine Rivers. (Camsell and Barbeau 1915, 249)

The name "Old Crow," however, is not a reference to Raven, but to Walking Crow, a respected former leader of the Kutchin.

Bering Strait Eskimo

"The Earth Diver" seems to make an appearance in a brief but significant statement by Edward W. Nelson, in his report on the Eskimo of Bering Strait, that "the creation of the earth and everything upon it is credited to the Raven Father . . . who is said to have come from the sky and made the earth when everything was covered with water" (Nelson 1899, 3). The following tale from Norton Sound is more of the Semitic deluge type. Nelson says "legends very similar to this are widely spread among Eskimo on the coast of Bering sea."

. . . In the first days the earth was flooded except a very high mountain in the middle. The water came up from the sea and covered all the land except the top of this mountain; only a few animals were saved, which escaped by going up the mountain side. A few people escaped by going into an umiak and subsisting on the fish they caught until the water subsided. Finally, as the waters lowered, the people who were saved went to live upon the mountains, eventually descending to the coast; the animals also came down and replenished the earth with their kind. During the flood the waves and currents cut the surface of the land into hollows and ridges, and then, as the water receded, it ran back into the sea, leaving the mountains and valleys as they are today. (Nelson 1899, 452)

Montagnais

> They say that there is one named Messou [Manabhozo], who restored
> the world when it was lost in the waters. . . . One day as he was out
> hunting an elk, his lynxes gave it chase even into the lake; and when
> they reached the middle of it, they were submerged in an instant.
> When he arrived there and sought his brothers everywhere, a bird told
> him that it had seen them at the bottom of the lake, and that certain
> animals or monsters held them there; but immediately the lake
> overflowed, and . . . drowned the whole earth. . . . He sent a raven to
> find a small piece of earth with which to build up another world. The
> raven was unable to find any, everything being covered with water. He
> made an otter dive. . . . At last a muskrat descended, and brought back
> some earth. (Alexander 1964, 42)

Thompson

Mankind is evil, so Beaver—also known as Louis or No'a (probably
derived from the Biblical Noah)—says that he will drown them in a
flood. He builds a great canoe for himself, his family, and a pair of
each kind of animal. The flood reaches to the tops of the mountains.
Eventually Beaver longs to see the earth again, and food is becoming
scarce, so he lets the water recede. He sends the Tsemok-bird, the
Eagle, and the Raven to find land. The first two are unsuccessful. The
Raven finds a little land but chooses to stay and eat corpses. Finally
the Ya'teayate-hawk returns with some leaves and twigs (Teit 1910,
333).

Dogrib or Slave

A great rain falls on the earth and covers the highest mountains.
Tchapewi builds a raft and places on it a pair of each type of animal.
He sends down several animals, including the otter, the beaver, and
the duck, but only the muskrat succeeds in bringing back a piece of
mud, which Tchapewi blows on to recreate the earth. Eventually the
earth can support the weight of a small bird, then that of a raven, and
finally it can support a fox (Petitot 1886, 317–18).

Gros Ventre

The god Nixant punishes mankind for its wickedness by making the earth crack open and water gush out, accompanied by rain. All animals perish except the Crow, while Nixant floats on buffalo chips. The Crow grows tired of floating about, so Nixant lets him rest several times on his pipe. Then Nixant unwraps the pipe, which contains animals. He sends the Large Loon and the Small Loon down to fetch mud, but they soon run out of breath. The Turtle is successful. After Nixant creates the earth, he sheds tears to create rivers (Kroeber 1908, 59–61).

Shoshone

> The whole earth was covered with water. Only on a high mountain there was a dry spot. Our Father sent the Crow to get earth in order to make our land. Then the Crow came back stinking. "You are crazy," said the Father; "you have eaten the drowned people. Now, go back, and go around homeless. You will eat whatever any one has killed. Go, now! you will be black." Then he said to the small birds, "Come, I will now hear which of you has a good heart and good sense." He found that the Chickadee was the only one that had any sense and was good-hearted. Then he bade it bring earth. It brought it. Our Father made the earth out of it. "It will be small," he said, "for little hands brought it. You will have six moons. You will not lose track of tongues. You have good thoughts." (Lowie 1909, 273)

Jicarilla Apache

After the deluge, several animals are sent out, but they became stuck in the mud. The crow is sent out. He discovers dry land but chooses to eat dead animals rather than return. The people grow angry and turn him black when he is finally brought back by Tornado (Dähnhardt [1907–12] 1970, 3: 71).

2 Raven Becomes Voracious

At the end of the incidents described in "The Birth of Raven," the boy (Raven) refuses to eat, and his parents are worried. The boy is advised to eat scabs (sometimes from his own body), and when he does so he becomes voracious, to the extent that he consumes all of the village's food supply and has to be sent away. The story is told by the Haida, Tsimshian, and Kwakiutl, as well as by the Tlingit (Boas [1916] 1970, 636–67).

3 The Theft of the Sun

The story of the acquisition of the sun is told with remarkable uniformity over most of the Northwest Coast (Boas [1916] 1970, 641–51; Teit 1919, 204–05; Birket-Smith and De Laguna 1938, 259–60; Osgood 1937, 183–84; McKennan 1959, 190–91), and sporadically north and east of that area, but there are a few interesting variations. It may be the sun that he steals, or the daylight, or the sun, moon, and stars. They may be in boxes, bundles, or balls. Raven may transform himself into a needle of hemlock, cedar, spruce, or fir, or he may become a blade of grass or a piece of dirt or down.

In southern British Columbia, the story becomes simplified: only the sun (in a box) remains, not the moon or stars, and among the Kwakiutl, Halkomelem, and Lillooet, the owner of the sun is Gull.

The "conception by eating" motif may be modified or missing. In a Kwakiutl version, Omeatl (Raven) hides in a piece of driftwood and then slips into the girl's body. The Squamish have a version in which Raven causes sea-urchin spines to stick into Gull's feet; Raven then asks for the sun box to be opened so that he can see well enough to pull out the spines (Boas [1916] 1970, 641–48).

Haida

In some Haida versions, Raven steals just the moon, rather than the stars, moon, and sun. He breaks the moon in half and makes the present moon out of one half, and the present sun out of the other half. The fragments may become the stars (Boas [1916] 1970, 651).

In a version that is typical of the Haida form, Raven travels north and transforms himself into a conifer needle, which is dipped up and swallowed by the chief's daughter:

> Not a long time after that she became pregnant. Then she gave birth [to a child], and its grandfather washed the child all over and put his feet to its feet. It began to creep about. After it had crept about for a while it cried so violently that no one could stop it. "Boo hoo, moon," it kept saying. After it had tired them out with its crying they stopped up the smoke hole, and, having pulled one box out of another four times, they gave it a round thing. There came light throughout the house. After it had played with this for a while it let it go and again started to cry. "Boo hoo, smoke hole," it cried. They then opened the smoke hole, and it cried again and said: "Boo hoo, more." And they made the space larger. Then he flew away with it. . . .
>
> He then put the moon into his armpit. . . .
>
> He came to a shore opposite some people who were fishing with fish rakes in Nass. And he said: "Hallo, throw one over to me. I will give you light." But they said: "Ha ha-a-a, he who is speaking is the one who is always playing tricks." He then let a small part shine and put it away again. They forthwith emptied their canoe in front of him several times. . . .
>
> He then bit off a part of the moon. After he had chewed it for a while he threw it up [into the sky]. "Future people are going to see you there in fragments forever." He then broke the moon into halves by throwing it down hard and threw [half of] it up hard into the air, the sun as well. (Swanton 1905, 116–18)

Bella Coola

A Bella Coola tale is quite interesting. It begins with a story some-times called "The Wall of Dawn," which appears in Siberia, but is found nowhere else in North America. "The Painting of the Birds" has been inserted in the middle of the following version.

> In the beginning there was no sun. A curtain was stretched be-

tween heaven and earth, so that here below it was always dark. Raven wanted to free the sun, but he could not. Then he went to the deities Masmasalaniq, Yulatimot (Heron), Matlapeeqock and Itlitlukak (according to others, Matlapalitsek) and asked them to free the sun. They tore the curtain and the sun began to light up the earth. However, it did not shine clearly and brightly, but only through a thick fog. Raven flew through the gap that the deities had made in heaven and found there an endless plain, that was inhabited by birds. Masmasalaniq and his brother wanted to paint them. Raven demanded to be painted first. Yulatimot painted him with bright colors, but he would not remain satisfied. Then Masmasalaniq painted him. Raven was no more satisfied with these colors than before. Thereupon Matlapeeqock painted him first, then Itliulak; none, however, could paint him properly. Then said Masmasalaniq, "Let us paint him black." They did so, but Raven cried, "It doesn't matter that I'm now ugly. I will now fly down to earth and tease and torment people." Then Masmasalaniq threw Raven down to earth. The four deities now painted all the birds and gave each of them his song and his skills. They assigned to them their seasons in which to sing, and in which to be silent.

Raven, however, was not satisfied with the sun, which shined so dimly, and decided to look for another. He flew over the whole world and finally came to the house of Chief Snq, who owned the Nusqemta (Place of Dawn). This was a round box with no cover or seam, in which there was the sun. The chief kept it in his house, where he hung it from a roof beam. Raven knew that the box could not be obtained by force, and contrived a trick. The chief had four daughters. The oldest used to dip water from a pool each morning. Raven turned himself into a pine needle and let himself fall into the bucket with which the girl collected water. When she drank the water, she swallowed the pine needle with it. She became pregnant and bore a child. As he grew up, he one day began to cry and would not be quieted. He cried for the Nusqemta. He rejected all food and cried endlessly, until the chief allowed him to play with it. But the next day he cried again, until the chief allowed him to take the Nusqemta out of the house, and to play with it in the street. He had scarcely left when he broke the box. The sun leaped out, and he flew away as Raven. (Boas 1895, 241–42)

Bering Strait Eskimo

Bering Strait Eskimo variants of "The Theft of the Sun" usually follow the general Northwest Coast format, though in one version it is Raven himself who hides the sun, and Raven's brother who is swallowed and reborn as the hero who brings back the sun, recalling the Tlingit variant in which Raven steals the sun from Raven-at-the-head-of-Nass (Nelson 1899, 461).

In the following story, from Paimut, on the lower Yukon, an important incident is missing: Raven's transformation into a small object that is swallowed by the sun-keeper's daughter to make her pregnant.

In the first days there was light from the sun and the moon as we now have it. Then the sun and the moon were taken away, and people were left on the earth for a long time with no light but the shining of the stars. The shamans made their strongest charms to no purpose, for the darkness of night continued.

In a village of the lower Yukon there lived an orphan boy who always sat upon the bench with the humble people over the entrance way in the kashim [men's house]. The other people thought he was foolish, and he was despised and ill-treated by everyone. After the shamans had tried very hard to bring back the sun and the moon but failed, the boy began to mock them, saying, "What fine shamans you must be, not to be able to bring back the light, when even I can do it."

At this the shamans became very angry and beat him and drove him out of the kashim. This poor orphan was like any other boy until he put on a black coat which he had, when he changed into a raven, preserving this form until he took off the coat again.

When the shamans drove the boy out of the kashim, he went to the house of his aunt in the village and told her what he had said to them and how they had beaten him and driven him out of the kashim. Then he said he wished her to tell him where the sun and the moon had gone, for he wished to go after them.

She denied that she knew where they were hidden, but the boy said, "I am sure you know where they are, for look at what a finely sewed coat you wear, and you could not see to sew it in that way if you did not know where the light is." After a long time he prevailed upon his aunt, and she said to him, "Well, if you wish to find the light you must take your snowshoes and go far to the south, to the place you will know when you get there."

The Raven boy at once took his snowshoes and set off for the south. For many days he traveled, and the darkness was always the same. When he had gone a very long way he saw far off in front of him a ray of light, and then he felt encouraged. As he hurried on the light showed again, plainer than before, and then vanished and appeared at intervals. At last he came to a large hill, one side of which was in a bright light while the other appeared in the blackness of night. In front of him and close to the hill the boy saw a hut with a man near by who was shovelling snow from the front of it.

The man was tossing the snow high in the air, and each time that he did this the light became obscured, thus causing the alternations of light and darkness which the boy had seen as he approached. Close beside the house he saw the light he had come in search of, looking like a large ball of fire. Then the boy stopped and began to plan how to secure the light and the shovel from the man.

After a time he walked up to the man and said, "Why are you throwing up the snow and hiding the light from our village?" The man stopped, looked up, and said, "I am only cleaning away the snow from my door; I am not hiding the light. But who are you, and whence did you come?" "It is so dark at our village that I did not like to live there, so I came here to live with you," said the boy. The man then said, "It is well; come into the house with me," and he dropped his shovel on the ground, and, stooping down, led the way through the underground passage into the house, letting the curtain fall in front of the door as he passed, thinking the boy was close behind him.

The moment the door flap fell behind the man as he entered, the boy caught up the ball of light and put it in the turned up flap of his fur coat in front; then, catching up the shovel in one hand, he fled away to the north, running until his feet became tired; then by means of his magic coat he changed into a raven and flew as fast as his wings would carry him. Behind he heard the frightful shrieks and cries of the old man, following fast in pursuit. When the old man saw that he could not overtake the Raven he cried out, "Never mind; you may keep the light, but give me my shovel."

To this the boy answered, "No; you made our village dark and you can not have your shovel," and Raven flew off, leaving him. As Raven travelled to his home he broke off a piece of the light and threw it away, thus making day. Then he went on for a long time in darkness and then threw out another piece of light, making it day again. This he continued to do at intervals until he reached the outside of the kashim in his own village and said, "Now, you good-for-nothing shamans, you see I have brought back the light, and it will be light and then dark so as to make day and night," and the shamans could not answer him. (Nelson 1899, 483–84)

Chipewyan

"The Theft of the Sun" is found as far east as Saskatchewan or Manitoba:

> White Bear . . . took down the sun. . . . Now, as everything was in darkness, the other animals could not hunt, and were starving. So they applied to the crow to get them out of their new trouble. In the mean time White Bear's daughter went for water, and as she was having a drink, something black was floating in the water, which she swallowed. Some days afterwards a child was born to her, and the infant grew so fast that soon he could walk about; and when he saw this bright thing . . . he began to cry for it. After much persuasion White Bear gave it to him to play with, but White Bear would not at first allow it. But as the child kept continually crying to be allowed to do so, he at last consented, but told him not to go far from camp, and if he saw anybody coming, to run into the tepee at once. This the child promised to do, but as soon as he got out, he threw the sun up into the sky, and flew away, for he was the crow in still another disguise. When the White Bear saw that he was cheated again by the crow, he was furious, and since then white bears have been always wicked. (Bell 1903, 79)

4 Raven Threatens to Let Out the Light

After Raven has obtained the sun or daylight, he comes upon people fishing. In the Tlingit versions, as we saw, Raven asks the fishermen to give him some fish, or he asks them to make less noise, or he asks to be taken across the river. They refuse, so he releases the sun, and the people run away and are transformed into the various animals. In a Tsimshian version, he again asks for fish and is refused, so he lets out the daylight, and the fishermen, who are frogs, drift to an island in the mouth of the river and become stone. In another Tsimshian version, the fishermen are ghosts. In the Haida versions, Raven asks for fish and is refused, but after Raven releases the moon (not the sun), there is no transformation of the fishermen into animals (Boas [1916] 1970, 649–50; Birket-Smith and De Laguna 1938, 260).

5 The Theft of Fresh Water

In the northern versions of this tale (Boas [1916] 1970, 651–53; cf. Teit 1919, 201–03; Birket-Smith and De Laguna 1938, 258–59), Raven asks for the fresh water but is refused, so after the owner of the water has slept, Raven makes him think he has soiled himself. The owner of the water may be Ganuk (Petrel), as in the Tlingit version, or it may be Eagle, or a chief or a woman. Raven may ask permission to sleep in the owner's house, and then put him to sleep by wishing it to happen, or he may tell the owner stories until he falls asleep. Sometimes Raven uses dog dung or chewed rotten cedar bark to convince the owner he has soiled himself. When the owner wakes up, Raven may steal the water when the owner goes out to wash the blanket, or he may threaten to tell on the owner if he is not given the water.

It is only in the Tlingit versions that Raven is turned black after he steals the water.

A different story is found further south, among the Heiltsuk, Kwakiutl, and Oweekeno. Raven puts ashes or cedar bark in his mouth, then goes to the owner of the water and asks for a drink. He is given a little, but he keeps asking for more, until his belly is full, or he secretly transfers the water to a bladder.

After Raven has stolen the water, he flies over the world, spitting it out to form rivers and streams. In some Kwakiutl and Nootka versions, however, he forms the rivers by urinating.

There are also references to a story or episode in which water can only be found at the roots of alder trees; in some cases it seems that the owner of fresh water had taken the water away from the earth, and it is only at the roots of alder trees that any water remains, but the story seems to be lost (Boas [1916] 1970, 653).

6 The Origin of Eulachon

Raven obtains one fish and smears the scales (or spawn or roe) of it over his canoe (or clothes), thus convincing the owner of all the eulachon that Raven has been catching some. In disgust at his own failure to keep them contained, the owner breaks down the barriers in his house and lets the rest of the eulachon out into the world. The Tlingit versions, as we have seen, begin with Raven causing two birds to start arguing with each other, after one of them has caught a fish. When one bird kicks the other in the belly, it vomits up a fish, and it is with the scales of this fish that Raven smears his canoe. In Tsimshian and Kwakiutl versions, the argument is between Raven and Gull (Boas [1916] 1970, 653–55). Other versions are found among the Tillamook, Tahltan, and Tanaina (Boas [1916] 1970, 652; Teit 1919, 203; Osgood 1937, 184).

Quite a different Tlingit and Haida story of the origin of fish is that Raven sees them floating on the ocean in a house or other receptacle, and he draws them in, often by a cane made out of two tentacles of an octopus (Boas [1916] 1970, 655–56).

7 The Origin of the Tides

Most versions of "The Origin of the Tides" resemble the Tlingit version. The tide turns only once every few days, and so it is hard for people to go out and gather food from the beach. Raven convinces the woman who owns the tides that he has managed to get some kind of sea food; in some cases, he uses spruce needles to convince her that he has gathered sea eggs (sea urchins). She asks him how he got the food. He torments her until she agrees to make the tide rise and fall more often. Besides the Tlingit versions, there are also variants among the Eyak, Tahltan, Haida, Nootka, Kwakiutl, and Oweekeno (Boas [1916] 1970, 656–57; Teit 1919, 201; Birket-Smith and De Laguna 1938, 250, 252, 261–62).

8 War with the South Wind

The South or Southeast Wind is blowing too hard. Raven and the other animals cannot go out to hunt, and their eyes are sore from the smoke that keeps blowing back into the houses. They get into a canoe and paddle to the Wind's house, but have difficulty landing because of the Wind's flatulence. They drive the Wind out of his house by biting him or by lighting a fire under him. He slips on Halibut and is caught and beaten. A compromise is reached, and the Wind agrees to alternate good weather with bad weather. The tale has been recorded among the Tsimshian, Haida, Kwakiutl, and Nootka (Boas [1916] 1970, 658–60; Hoebel 1941 *passim*).

9 The Theft of Fire

The story of Raven and "The Theft of Fire" is very popular; it is found among the Tlingit, Haida, Tsimshian, Tahltan, Bella Coola, Oweekeno, Kwakiutl, Nootka, and Comox (Boas [1916] 1970, 661–62; Teit 1919, 218), and more isolated "fire" stories involving a raven or crow occur further south and east. In other parts of North America and the Old World, some other character may have the principal role. In the following tales, Raven (or "the raven" or "the crow") plays various roles: leader, follower, winner, loser. Secondary motifs are often added, such as his transformation from white to black.

On the Northwest Coast, the general pattern is as follows. Fire is kept on an island, in a house, in "the village of the animals," or at the bottom of the sea. Raven sends several animals to get it, but they are unsuccessful. Most often it is the deer who finally succeeds, or Raven dressed in a deer skin. Pitch wood is tied to the deer's tail, and he goes to the owner of the fire and puts his tail in the fire, which is why deer (i.e., mule deer) now have short black tails. The tail catches fire, and he runs off. He strikes trees with his tail, which is why fire can be obtained from wood. In some versions belonging to the Haida, Tsimshian, and Chilcotin, as with one of the Tlingit versions, it is Raven himself who obtains the fire. It is sometimes said that Raven put fire into stones as well as trees, which is why both stones and fire drills can be used to obtain fire.

Yurok

> At first they had no fire. . . . They said, "We want that. Where did you see it? He said, "I saw fire in the sky." So they gathered and planned and went to the sky, to buy the fire. But he who had it, Sun, would not sell it. They continued trying to buy it, but he would not sell, he said.
>
> When they found that they could not buy it from him, they began to confer again. They said, "We must have it. Let us begin to gamble. We will play at the house where it is, and one of us will sit at every short distance, along the path." This path was the one by which Fire-Owner (Sun) went to his house when he travelled during the day. . . . The one who was to do the gambling, Raven, said: "When you hear me singing, tell the one next to you, and he to the next one, to be ready, because it will be as if I were telling them that I am about to snatch fire." . . . When Raven began to sing, all knew that he was about to seize fire, and they became ready. Then he snatched it and passed it to the Fishers. Fire-Owner followed. The fire kept travelling, one handing it to the next, Fire-Owner close behind. When Round Rock got it, he rolled down the long hill and gained. At the foot of the hill another one took it and passed it on to Turtle, who clutched it in his hand and dived, just as Fire-Owner came up. Under the water, turtle rubbed fire on willow roots until it had all gone out. Thus they obtained fire.
>
> Now when they had the fire, the woge [spirits] came together and began to question how they would extract it. One said, "I think we shall get it out of the willow roots. Let us make one of them flat, the other round and long." So they made the fire drill like that. (Kroeber 1976, 441–42)

Pawnee

The "first people" arrive at the Missouri River. They have no fire. They want to get it from the sun, so they send the swallow. The swallow fails and burns his beak in the process. They send the crow, who also fails and is turned from white to black. A third (unidentified) bird succeeds (Dähnhardt [1907–12] 1970, 3: 102).

Cherokee

In the beginning there is no fire, but Thunderbird sends lightning and puts fire into the base of a sycamore on an island. The raven flies to the fire but only manages to burn his feathers black. The owls and snakes also fail, but finally the spider makes a round vessel from his thread, swims across, and brings back a coal (Mooney 1900, 240–42).

10 The Origin of Humans; The Origin of Death

The following Tsimshian story is obviously related to the Tlingit one in which Raven tries to create humans out of stones and leaves:

> Txamsem [Giant; Raven] went along up Nass River, and came to the place where Stone and Elderberry Bush were quarreling, discussing who should give birth first. Stone wished to give birth first, and Elderberry Bush also wished to give birth first. Txamsem listened to what they were saying. Stone said, "If I give birth first, then people will live a long time; if you give birth first, people will live a short time." Giant went to the place were they were and looked, and behold! Stone had almost given birth to her child. Then he went to Elderberry Bush and touched her. He said, "give birth first, Elderberry Bush." Then Elderberry Bush gave birth to a child. For that reason people do not live many years. Because Elderberry Bush gave birth to her child first, man dies quickly. If Stone had given birth first, it would not be so. That is what our people say. That is the story of Elderberry Bush's children; and therefore the Indians are much troubled because Stone did not give birth to her children first. For this reason the people die soon, and elderberry bushes grow on their

graves. (Boas [1916] 1970, 62)

In a Tahltan version, it is said that people must die because Tree and Rock were both pregnant once, but the child of Rock died, while the child of Tree lived (Teit 1919, 216; cf. 206–07).

Haida

The Haida have a completely different account of the origin of people:

> At that time the Raven traveled all over the earth, and one day he found a cockle which was being thrown about by the waves. He heard a noise inside the shell. He went near to see what it was. He hid near by and discovered many children in the cockleshell. He opened it and found many people. (Swanton 1905, 320)

There are several versions of this Haida tale. Sometimes it is only certain families that originate from the clamshell. Generally, either Raven finds a clamshell filled with people and perhaps animals, or he marries a clam who gives birth to people (Boas [1916] 1970, 631–33).

The Haida and Oweekeno ascribe the origin of death to an event described below in "Raven Burns a Girl's Groins": Raven's son returns, but he looks different, and so Raven sends him away.

Bering Strait Eskimo

> It was in the time when there were no people on the earth plain. During four days the first man lay coiled up in the pod of a beach-pea (L. maritimus). On the fifth day he stretched out his feet and burst the pod, falling to the ground, where he stood up, a full-grown man. . . . When he looked up again he saw approaching . . . a dark object. . . . This was a raven, and, as soon as it stopped, it raised one of its wings, pushed up its beak, like a mask, to the top of its head, and changed at once into a man. . . . At last [Raven] said: "What are you? Whence did you come?" . . . To this the Man replied: "I came from the pea-pod." . . . "Ah!" exclaimed Raven, "I made that vine, but did

Raven post representing Raven killing the salmon. Upper figure, raven in human form; bird head, Raven as teller of lies; large face in center, personified jade adze; bottom figure, the salmon Raven killed (Tlingit). *Photograph courtesy of the Royal British Columbia Museum, Victoria, British Columbia, PN1622.*

not know that anything like you would ever come from it." (Nelson 1899, 452–53)

Maya

The gods try three times to create humans but are unable to imbue them with life. For the fourth attempt, they ask the wildcat, the coyote, the parrot, and the crow to bring white and yellow maize, and with this they are able to create animate human beings (*Popol Vuh* 3.1).

This Mayan tale is probably not related to any Northwest Coast tale. But it is interesting to note that the crow plays a part in the diffusion of agricultural myths (corresponding to the Neolithic fertility myths of the Old World) from Central America to New England. (Agriculture was mainly transmitted northward.) The Indians of Rhode Island never killed crows, even though they raided the maize fields, because it was said to be the crow who had brought them, from the southwest, a kernel of maize in one ear and a bean in the other (Roger Williams [1643] 1973, 174).

11 The Painting of the Birds

Among the Tlingit, Haida, and Tsimshian, the blackening of the crows is often part of "The Killing of the Salmon." But the real "Painting of the Birds" occurs among the Kwakiutl, Bella Coola, Comox, Tahltan, and Chipewyan, although versions without Raven are found among the Halkomelem, Quinault, and Chinook (Boas [1916] 1970, 664–65, 677–78; Teit 1919, 208–09). The story is very widespread among the Eskimo, although in the Eskimo versions there are usually only two characters.

The basic story is that Raven and another bird decide to paint each other, perhaps to make themselves more beautiful. The two birds argue, and Raven is then painted black. In the Kwakiutl version, the raven character is duplicated: Omeatl (himself generally identified with Raven) paints most of the birds, then rubs coal over the raven, and clay over the sea gull (Boas [1916] 1970, 665). We have seen the Bella Coola form of "The Painting of the Birds" in their version of

"The Theft of the Sun." The Eskimo forms are typified by the following variant:

> The owl and the raven were fast friends. One day the raven made a new dress, dappled white and black, for the owl, who in return made a pair of boots of whalebone for the raven, and then began to make a white dress. When she was about to try it on, the raven was hopping about and would not sit still. The owl got angry. . . . As the raven continued hopping about, the owl fell into a passion and poured the contents of her lamp over him. Then the raven cried "qaq! qaq!" and since that day he has been black all over. (Boas 1888, 641)

12 The Origin of Fog

Raven visits Eagle, Petrel, or Gull and asks him how long he has lived. The other bird gives an answer that indicates he has lived a very long time. Raven replies that he himself has lived much longer; in some versions, he says he has existed since before the world was made. The other bird takes off his hat and pushes Raven's canoe away. A fog arises, and Raven is forced to admit that the other is older, or more powerful. The other puts his hat back on, and the fog disappears. Besides being a Tlingit story, it is also told by the Haida, Tsimshian, Kwakiutl, Tahltan, and Comox (Boas [1916] 1970, 666; Teit 1919, 212–13).

13 The Origin of Salmon

It is natural that the Northwest Coast Indians should have some stories about the origin of salmon, since it was the mainstay of their economy. The Tahltan say that the salmon were in the sea but would not go up the rivers, so Raven put a salmon egg in each of the rivers, so that the salmon must go up them each year (Teit 1919, 206), but the usual story is more complex. According to Boas, the story actually consists of four sub-plots. The order can vary, or a sub-plot can be missing.

(a) Raven Carves Salmon Out of Various Kinds of Wood

In a Bella Coola, Oweekeno, and Kwakiutl story, Raven attempts to carve a salmon out of wood, or he has someone else carve it for him, but the salmon does not come to life. It may be that the skin and bones are too tough, or that it cannot swim. In the Kwakiutl version, Raven throws the wooden fish into a stream, but instead of swimming upstream, it goes out to sea and becomes a halibut (Boas [1916] 1970, 666–67).

(b) Raven Marries the Dead Twin

In many cultures, it is believed that twins have special powers, and the people of the Northwest Coast believe they have power over the salmon.

The Kwakiutl and Oweekeno tell a story in which Raven goes to some graves and tries to find a grave of twins. A voice from one grave says, "I used to be a salmon." Raven opens the grave and finds a woman, whom he washes with the water of life. He asks her to create salmon, and she does so, by one of several different means. She may swim in the river, which becomes full of salmon; she may put her little finger in the river, after which a salmon swims upstream; or she may wash her hands to produce a salmon. The process is repeated several times, and the salmon increase in numbers.

In some versions, Raven goes away for a while, and she secretly creates salmon in his absence and feeds it to other people. Raven returns and sees a piece of salmon stuck in someone's teeth, so he asks the woman to create more salmon (Boas [1916] 1970, 667–68).

(c) Raven and the Salmon Woman

Raven finds a beautiful woman, sometimes called Cloud Woman or Bright-Cloud Woman. In a Bella Coola version, Raven goes to the Salmon country, and his sisters make holes in the canoes of the salmon people so that they cannot be followed. Raven asks the chief's daughter to help him carry food into the canoe, and when she steps into the boat, he carries her off. As with some versions of "Raven

Marries the Dead Twin," the salmon woman is at first unwilling to produce salmon, but she feeds salmon to other people when Raven is away. Raven asks her to produce more salmon, and she does so, generally by washing her hands in water.

In some versions, the Salmon Woman offers to make Raven more beautiful by giving him long hair. He becomes proud and arrogant. One day his hair gets caught on some of the many salmon that are drying inside his house. He scolds them, and this constitutes an insult to his wife, so she and the salmon disappear. In the Tlingit version, as we saw, he beats his wife. In a Tsimshian version, he has bad luck at gambling, and he accuses his wife of being unfaithful to him and thereby causing his bad luck.

Other versions of this story are told by the Haida, Oweekeno, Kwakiutl, Chilcotin, and Shuswap (Boas [1916] 1970, 668–71).

(d) Raven Abducts the Daughter of the Salmon Chief

Raven finally manages to obtain salmon permanently, by abducting the daughter of the Salmon Chief. This episode often follows the loss of his twin wife. Raven goes to the country of the Salmon Chief. Raven's sister (or sisters) makes holes in the Salmon People's canoes (as in the Bella Coola version of "Raven and the Salmon Woman"). In the Oweekeno version, the Salmon Chief tells his four daughters to swim in the sea. When they return, each is carrying a salmon. The salmon are cooked, and the Salmon Chief tells the guests to throw the bones into the fire. The nose of one of the girls begins to bleed, and it is because Raven has hidden one of the bones in his mouth.

The "stolen bone" scene can occur in other places. In one Kwakiutl version, a chieftainess tells her daughters to go swimming. When they do, they turn into salmon. Their clothes are also thrown into the water, but Omeatl (Raven) steals a blanket pin, so when the girls come out of the water, one is missing a collar bone. The story usually finishes with one of the daughters helping Raven to put supplies in his canoe, at which point he grabs her and paddles off, with the Salmon People in pursuit.

There is another Kwakiutl version:

And Omeatl thought about how to obtain the salmon again. Finally he decided to steal Maisila, the daughter of Ma, the Salmon. But she was already married to Halqseoalis (Killer Whale). Omeatl got into his canoe and put his paddle into the water twice. Then the boat went all by itself to Ma's country. He got out and saw Ma's slave busy felling a tree by himself. Omeatl slipped unseen into the tree and bit off the end of the wedge that the slave had driven into the tree. The slave was annoyed and took a new wedge. Omeatl bit this one off also, and he did the same to a third and a fourth. Then the slave was upset and wept and cried, "Oh, my master will beat me because his wedges are broken!" Omeatl now came out of the tree, walked up to the slave as if he had just arrived, and said, "Don't cry, I will help you." He took the wedges and held them in his mouth, and in this way put the tips back on. Then he struck the tree once only and felled it himself and split it into logs as it fell. Then he spoke to the slave: "Doesn't Maisila live here? I want to have her for my wife. You must help me to get her." The slave promised to bring him secretly into the house while Halqseoalis was out hunting. He let him hide in the boat under the logs, and went off to the house. In the evening the slave and Maisila brought the wood into the house. Omeatl slipped into a log that the woman carried, and on the way he put his arm around her body. This frightened her and she threw the log away in terror. But since she saw nothing, she thought she had been deceived, and she picked it up again. Soon, however, Omeatl embraced her again, and again she threw the piece of wood away. Four times this happened, then she went into the house, and Omeatl followed her unnoticed into her room. But when Halqseoalis returned to the house the following morning, Omeatl put on his raven cloak and flew up onto the totem pole in front of the house.

Then Halqseoalis noticed him and invited him to come in. Omeatl accepted his invitation. When he sat by the fire, Halqseoalis asked him where he came from. He didn't answer these questions, but only said, "Why do you have such a big belly? Come here and let me make you slender and handsome." Halqseoalis was afraid and at first did not want to go to him, but Omeatl knew how to speak convincingly. Then Omeatl cut his belly open and took out his stomach so that he died. He did the same thing to his three brothers, who had returned with him from the hunt.

Then he took the young woman, set her in his boat, and went back to his own country. Ma sent out all of his boats to pursue the robber, but they didn't catch him. When he was near his own country, Omeatl changed them all into salmon and assigned each of them to a river. So it happens that one now finds salmon in all the waters. And Omeatl taught men to catch and dry salmon. One small fish, called hanuq, swam right behind Omeatl's boat as he was fleeing. His eyes were pushed close together by Omeatl. (Boas 1895, 175)

The Bella Coola, Oweekeno, and Chilcotin have their own versions of the abduction story (Boas [1916] 1970, 671–74).

TRICKSTER TALES

14 Raven Kills the Salmon

In a highly variable story told by the Tsimshian, Haida, and Kwakiutl, as well as by the Tlingit (Boas [1916] 1970, 675–76), Raven sees a salmon jumping in a river. He tricks the salmon into being killed, and the trick involves making four holes and then daring the salmon to jump against Raven and knock him down. The salmon knocks Raven over and falls into a hole. Raven tries to catch the salmon but cannot. This is repeated three times, but on the fourth attempt, Raven manages to catch the salmon when it falls into the hole (Boas [1916] 1970, 675).

After Raven kills the salmon, he cooks it, and the next part of the tale includes an episode in which the crows are turned black. In the Tsimshian version, Raven cooks the salmon and sends the crows to fetch dishes. They repeatedly bring only seashells, so he goes himself to find proper wooden dishes. The crows eat the salmon while he is away, so he turns them black. In the Haida version, it is again the crows rather than (as in the Tlingit version) Raven who actually eat the salmon. They put some of the salmon in his mouth while he sleeps, but he is not deceived. He spits in their faces and turns them black.

The Tahltan and Eyak have simpler versions of the story (Teit

1919, 205–06; Birket-Smith and De Laguna 1938, 249, 252–53, 261).

15 The Killing of Grizzly Bear

Raven invites Bear to go fishing with him. Before they go, Raven catches one salmon, and cuts off part of it to use as bait, but he does not let Bear know what he is doing. When they are out on the water, Bear asks him what he is using for bait, and he claims that he is using his own testicles. He urges Bear to do likewise, and Bear reluctantly castrates himself, or he allows Raven to perform the operation, and Bear dies. (At this point, Raven tears out Cormorant's tongue.)

When they get back to shore, Raven tells Bear's wife (or wives) that Bear has fainted, and that she must eat some red-hot stones to bring her husband luck. In other versions, he says that her husband is away making some new hooks, and that she and Raven should eat. He fills halibut stomachs with red-hot stones and says that it is customary to swallow the stomachs whole. She does so, and he sends Cormorant for water. When Bear's wife drinks the water, the steam kills her.

The story belongs to the Tsimshian, Haida, Tahltan, Kwakiutl, and Nootka, as well as the Tlingit, and fairly similar forms occur among the Interior Salish and the Eyak (Boas [1916] 1970, 680–83; Teit 1919, 208–09; Birket-Smith and De Laguna 1938, 266–67).

16 Cormorant's Tongue Is Torn Out

There are two forms of the story in which Cormorant loses his tongue. In the first form (found among the Tlingit, Haida, and Nootka), Raven has gone fishing with Bear and Cormorant and has killed Bear. In order to prevent Cormorant from telling Bear's wife or wives, he pulls a louse off Cormorant's head, and then tells Cormorant to bite the louse. When Cormorant opens his mouth, Raven tears out his tongue. In a Nootka version, Cormorant asks for some of the gum that Raven is chewing, and Raven tears out his tongue after pretending to put some gum in the other bird's mouth.

In the other form of the story (found among the Tlingit, Haida,

Tsimshian, and Kwakiutl), the winning and losing roles are at first reversed. Raven goes fishing with Cormorant, and Cormorant keeps catching more fish than Raven. Raven uses the trick with the louse to pull out Cormorant's tongue, and then he turns the fishes' heads towards himself. When they get back to shore, Raven claims that he caught all the fish, and Cormorant cannot speak to defend his rights. Raven claims that Cormorant lost his voice while they were fishing, or that Cormorant had put a hook in his mouth and pulled out his own tongue (Boas [1916] 1970, 678–80).

In a Tahltan story, Raven uses the "louse" trick to pull out the tongue of the gossiping Crow (Teit 1919, 222–23).

17 The Killing of Pitch

Raven asks Pitch to go fishing with him. Pitch is reluctant to fish in the daytime, but is eventually persuaded to do so. He begins to melt in the sun, and he asks to go home. In some versions, Raven tells him to lie under a mat, and in other versions Raven pretends to paddle home, but he is putting his paddle in the water edgewise. Pitch melts in the sun. The story is told by the Tsimshian, Haida, Tahltan, Oweekeno, Kwakiutl, and Halkomelem, as well as by the Tlingit (Boas [1916] 1970, 683–84; Teit 1919, 210).

18 Raven's Beak Is Torn Off

In a story told in very similar versions by the Tlingit, Kwakiutl, Tahltan, and Eyak (Boas [1916] 1970, 684–85; Teit 1919, 224; Birket-Smith and De Laguna 1938, 249), Raven steals bait off people's hooks, but he gets his beak caught on a hook. They haul the line in, and Raven braces himself against the bottom of the canoe. His beak is torn off. He makes himself a new beak out of bark and pitch, and goes looking for his real beak, which is being kept on a wall; the people think it is the nose of a monster. Raven asks to see it, and when he does, he grabs it and flies off. In other versions, he tells the people that the presence of the nose means that an enemy is approaching. When the people leave, Raven steals their provisions.

In a Kutchin version, it is merely said that his beak is taken away from him, and he uses various tricks to get it back (Boas [1916] 1970, 685).

19 Raven Is Swallowed by a Whale

Raven sees a whale out at sea, and asks the whale to swallow him, or he flies into the whale's mouth. In some stories, Raven is accompanied by Mink, or Mink may take the place of Raven. When the whale opens its mouth, fish pour in, and Raven lives on these fish for a while. Later he begins eating the whale's fat, and eventually he eats the whale's heart, and the whale dies. Raven wishes the whale would drift ashore, and it does so. Raven cries out, until some people cut open the whale, and Raven flies out unseen. When the people have finished converting the whale's fat to oil, Raven returns and asks them if they had heard or seen anything before they cut open the whale, and when they say they have, he tells them that it is an evil omen, indicating that they will be attacked, or visited by a disease. They leave, and he takes their provisions.

The story is very widespread: the Eskimo, Tlingit, Haida, Nootka, Eyak, Tanana, Comox, Oweekeno, and Quileute all tell the tale (Boas [1916] 1970, 687–89; Birket-Smith and De Laguna 1938, 265; McKennan 1959, 192–93; Andrade 1931, 46–47).

20 Raven Travels with His Slave

Other Northwest Coast forms of this tale are very similar to that of the Tlingit. Raven creates a slave, who is to be his "speaker," and Raven pretends to be an important chief. The slave is told to tell people that Raven is the chief who wears abalone-shell ear-ornaments, but the slave keeps telling people that the ornaments are made out of cockle shells. In a Haida version, Raven hangs salmon heads from his nose and tells his slave to say that they are weasels, but the slave disobeys.

In the second part of the tale, Raven is offered food, but the slave keeps saying that Raven is not hungry, and so Raven must go without food.

Raven decides to pretend to die. His "death" is to occur after some fish oil drops into his eye. He tells his slave to tell the people that they must leave. The slave, however, ties up the box into which Raven is placed, so that when everyone has left, the slave gets to eat, and Raven must starve again.

In the fourth part of the tale, Raven and his slave go to a canyon. Raven places something across the canyon: a stem of skunk cabbage, a piece of kelp, or a stalk of wild celery (cow parsnip). Raven crosses the canyon easily and insists that the slave cross also. The slave is afraid that the bridge will not hold him, but eventually he makes the attempt. The bridge breaks or twists, and the slave plunges to his death. Raven pretends to mourn the slave, but cuts him open and eats the contents of his stomach.

The tale is told, in whole or in part, by the Tsimshian, Haida, and Kwakiutl, but the most extensive forms are found among the Tlingit (Boas [1916] 1970, 689–91).

21 Raven Gathers Poor Food

Besides the Tlingit versions, there are Haida, Heiltsuk, and Eyak variants of this tale. Raven and a companion go gathering food, but Raven gets only poor food. In one version, Raven gets fish that are dry, while his companion's fish are very fat. Raven announces that he is going off into the woods, but he tells Eagle that if a stump should arrive, he should rub its face with black cod. Raven arrives, disguised as a stump, and Eagle rubs its face with red-hot stones. When Raven comes back later, with his face blackened, he says that some bark fell on him. In another version, Raven is disguised as a log, and Eagle strikes the log (Boas [1916] 1970, 692; Boas 1932, 17; Birket-Smith and De Laguna 1938, 250–51, 262–64).

In many cases, it is said that the fish that Raven and his companion are finding are ones that have been left stranded after the lowering of the water in "The Deluge" or in "The Origin of the Tides."

22 Raven Becomes a Woman

There are also only Tlingit and Haida versions of this tale. In the Haida version, Raven takes the form of a woman, and transforms a stone into a child. The killer whales come along, and Raven marries one of them. In the canoe, Raven insists that her child is hungry, but when the killer whales give Raven some seal meat, she secretly eats it herself. When she lives with the killer whales, she gets into the habit of consuming the fish oil at night. One day, her labret is found in the oil, and Raven's excuse is that the labret has the habit of wandering off by itself. The killer whales notice that Raven has a tail, but she says that it is not so unusual. The Haida versions, however, do not conclude with Raven's killing of the whales (Boas [1916] 1970, 692–94).

23 The Bungling Host

"The Bungling Host," with or without Raven, is a story of immense popularity across North America, and Boas summarizes it thus:

> There are a number of distinct types of these tales, each of which shows a characteristic distribution. Perhaps the most widely spread type of these tales is the one in which it is described how the host takes a part of his own body, which he cuts out or pulls out, or obtains in some other manner, and which he uses for treating his visitor. On the North Pacific coast this type occurs particularly in the form of the seal or bear heating his hands in front of the fire, and letting oil drip out of them into a dish; and in the other one, in which a bird, generally the kingfisher or a related water bird, strikes his ankle with a stone, and takes out a salmon egg, which he proceeds to boil, thus preparing a dish for his guest. . . . The tale having the widest distribution is that of the Fish Hawk or Kingfisher, who jumps into the water, diving for fish. This occurs practically over the whole of North America, apparently with the sole exception of the northern part of the North Pacific coast. ([1916] 1970, 694–95)

Boas also says, of the "Diving for Fish" version, that "it appears almost regularly in a highly specialized form, there being a hole in the ice, and a host diving in this hole. . . . On the North Pacific coast the animal simply dives into the water" ([1916] 1970, 699).

The story is usually told in the form of three or four similar tales, one after another: Raven (or some other main character) goes to visit each person in turn; the host magically produces food, and Raven makes a fool of himself when he attempts to duplicate the feat.

Nootka

> Bear invited Raven to a feast. He made a big fire, put a bowl nearby and held his hands over it. Fat dripped from his hands into the bowl. Then he roasted a salmon, which he served to Raven with the fat. Afterwards Raven invited the Bear. When the latter went to Raven's house, he laughed because he knew that Raven would try to imitate him. Raven made a big fire, set a bowl near it and held his hands over it. He turned them and shook them, but no fat ran out. He only managed to burn his hands. So now the raven has black wings and feet. (Boas 1895, 106)

The Comox have a version in which Anan (a small bird) invites all the animals for a feast. He puts a hook in his behind and pulls out some mountain-goat fat. Later Raven tries to do the same thing, but only manages to make himself bleed. Then Mamelaquitsa invites all the animals to a feast, cuts his leg, and lets fish eggs drop out. Raven tries to imitate him but only produces blood. Finally Seal invites the animals to a feast, holds his hands over the fire, and lets oil drip out. Raven tries to do the same, but blisters his hands instead (Boas 1895, 77).

In a Kwakiutl version, there are again three hosts that Raven tries to imitate. Waqwaqoli hits his behind and produces berries, but when Raven tries to imitate him he produces excrement. Kileqoitsa (a river bird) cuts his foot, and salmon comes out; when Raven tries to imitate him, he produces his own blood. Finally Seal invites the animals and holds his hands over a fire to produce oil, but when Raven tries to imitate him he burns his fingers (Boas 1895, 177).

Raven occurs in "The Bungling Host" as far south as the territory of the Quileute (Andrade 39–45, 109–115).

24 The Visit to Shadow Town

Raven sees a house that is inhabited by shadows or ghosts. The house is full of fish, and he helps himself. Finally he tries to carry some of the provisions out of the house. In some versions he is then beaten with wedges or a hammer, while in other versions he is beaten with sticks. Besides the Tlingit, Haida, Tahltan, and Bella Coola versions, there are also Chinook, Tillamook, and Takelma versions further south, but without Raven as the central character (Boas [1916] 1970, 702–23; Teit 1919, 225).

25 Raven Kills Deer

In the Tlingit and Haida versions of this tale, Raven invites Deer to accompany him when he goes to split wood. He asks Deer to hold the wedges, but then strikes Deer on the head with the hammer. In the Kwakiutl and Oweekeno versions, Raven and Deer talk about who is the older, or who has the most worthy ancestors. Then Raven kills him. In a Nootka version, Raven takes Deer to a precipice. Raven asks him to join him in mourning for their ancestors. Raven tells him that he is not mourning properly and asks him to close his eyes and lift his head, at which point Raven kills him. In a Comox version, Raven and Deer are again on a cliff. They argue about their wealth, and Raven pushes Deer over a cliff, but when Raven goes down to eat him, people have already butchered Deer, and Raven is left with nothing but the intestines (Boas [1916] 1970, 703–04). There are also Heiltsuk, Eyak, and Quileute versions (Boas 1932, 18; Birket-Smith and De Laguna 1938, 266; Andrade 1931, 31–32, 105–09).

And finally we have some tales that are not found among the Tlingit and hence could not be discussed in chapter 1.

26 Raven Steals Salmon Eggs

People put salmon eggs into a canoe. Raven pretends to be sick or injured, and is put in the canoe with the eggs. As the people paddle along, Raven's mother or sister smells something and asks what it is, and Raven replies that it is a scab that he has been scratching; or the bilge-water becomes white, and Raven claims that it is matter coming from his wound. In fact, however, he has been eating all the eggs. The story is found only among the Haida (Boas [1916] 1970, 705).

27 Raven Steals His Sisters' Berries

Raven and his sisters go gathering berries. When the berries have been collected, Raven gets his excrements to call like warriors, and Raven tells his sisters to hide in the woods. When they have gone, he eats all the berries. When they come back, he says that the berries have been stolen and that he has been beaten up. They discover that he has been lying, and they give him a real beating. The tale is told by the Kwakiutl, Nootka, Bella Coola, Oweekeno, Comox, and Lillooet (Boas [1916] 1970, 705).

28 Raven Burns a Girl's Groins

(a) Raven and the Girl

At one time Omeatl [Raven] sat by the fire, and opposite him there was a beautiful girl, whose name was Kokotsaqsmalekat (*Merganser serrator*). Her skin was white as snow. He would have liked to have her as a wife, but she wanted to have nothing to do with him. Then he thought of a trick. He said to her, "You haven't bathed for so long, you should take a bath." "Fine," she replied, "then make a fire for me." Then she went into her room and washed her whole body. But Omeatl flew into the woods. He went to the cedar and asked it, "What do you do when people throw you in the fire?" The cedar answered, "I cry. The people call it crackling." Raven replied, "Then I can't use you." He flew to the yellow cedar and asked it what it did when one threw it into the fire. It answered, "I cry and jump up high." Then Raven said, "That's fine. I'm going to throw you into the fire, and a beautiful girl will sit near you. Jump right into her lap and burn her." Raven carried the wood to the house and made a fire, and Kokotsaqsmalekat sat there to dry herself. Then the wood sprang up high and burned her lap. Raven pitied her and said, "I know a good remedy. Go into the woods, and when you see a plant out there, a stem without leaves, that moves up and down, then sit right on it, and you will be healed right away." The girl followed his advice. Hardly had she walked out of the house, when Raven flew into the woods, hid himself under the foliage, and let only his penis stick out. The girl came and did what Raven had ordered. But then she saw Omeatl's sparkling eyes and realized he had deceived her. She grabbed him and beat him until he lay there nearly dead. (Boas 1895, 178–79)

This is a Kwakiutl version of the story, but there are similar versions from the Haida, Tahltan, Nootka, Bella Coola, Oweekeno, Comox, and Chilcotin (Boas [1916] 1970, 707–08; Teit 1919, 206–07). The girl is often Raven's sister, daughter, or step-daughter. This part of the story is often followed by a second, which is more variable but goes somewhat as follows.

(b) The Thunderbird Abducts Raven's Son

The above story continues with Raven putting some of the secretion from the girl's vagina into a pair of clam shells, which give birth to a boy, who grows quickly. The boy is carried away by Thunderbird, or other supernatural beings, because Raven used to make fun of them. When the boy comes back, he looks different, and Raven refuses to recognize him as his son and sends him away. According to the Haida and Oweekeno, this is the cause of death in the world.

The story is Haida, Kwakiutl, and Oweekeno, but a Comox story is similar (Boas [1916] 1970, 707–10; Boas 1932, 14–16).

29 The Master Fisherman

Haida

Raven wanted to get possession of a woman who was already married. So he decided to get rid of her husband with a trick. He went to an island that he owned and returned with the skin of a robin [i.e., flicker]. He went to where he knew the man would be and carried the bird skin right in view to call the man's attention to it. This attracted his attention, and he said, "I've always wanted feathers like that, where did you get the bird skin?" Raven replied, "Yes, if you tie the feathers to your hook, you will catch a lot of fish. Here! I'll give them to you!" The other was glad and would have liked to have more feathers. Raven continued, "On my island there are many birds of this sort. Let's go tomorrow and we can shoot some." The man invited Raven into his house for the night and entertained him well. Raven ate up all the provisions of his host. Early in the morning they left. When they arrived at the island, Raven said, "I will go ashore first and see where the birds are." His companion agreed. Raven went ashore, and the other waited for him to return. Raven plucked some willow twigs and changed them into robins, which he carried to the boat. "See," he cried, "how many birds I've found." The other became very eager to go ashore and try his luck. Meanwhile Raven sat down in the back of the boat and pretended to fall asleep. He thought continually, "Oh, if only the wind would start to blow my boat away from the island!" The man soon noticed and called to Raven, "The boat is drifting away, paddle it back!" But the other acted as if he didn't hear, and when he was far enough away, he paddled to the house of the man that he had left alone on the island. Before he arrived, he took the form of this man and sat down by the spring from which the wife always drew water. It wasn't long before she came for water. Raven pretended not to see her, and said to himself, "Oh, how badly Raven has treated me," and then he turned to the woman and asked her for halibut and fish oil, until he could eat no more. Then he said to the woman, "We will go to sleep now, and afterwards we shall eat some more."

The man whom he had left alone on the island to perish was very worried. But suddenly he remembered his magic fish club and thought, "If only I had the club here." It immediately arrived and carried him home. He sat by the spring, and, when his wife came to fetch water, she heard about everything that had happened. The rescued man kept himself hidden, but ordered his wife to close up all cracks and chinks in the house. When she had carried out these orders, he came inside, caught Raven, who could not escape, and beat him half to death. He threw him out of the door onto the place where people went to urinate. In the following morning the wife went out to urinate, and she sat right above Raven. Then he cried, "Your genitals are all red." When the man heard this, he took him again and beat him half to death. Then he threw him into the branches and started a big fire under him. He fed the fire all day, but Raven wasn't dead. When [the man] got up the following morning, he saw [Raven] sitting in the fire. Then he again beat him half to death and threw him onto the place on the beach that served as a latrine, at the foot of a great rock. When the tide came, the water washed Raven away. He thought, when the water carried him around, "Oh, I wish my relatives would come and find me!" What he wished for happened. A boat came, in which his relatives were sitting, and they took him away. (Boas 1895, 310)

The tale is told by the Haida, Heiltsuk, and Coast Salish (Boas [1916] 1970, 710–11; Chowning n.d., 40).

30 War with the Thunderbird

This rather variable tale pits the main character, who may or may not be Raven, against Thunderbird or Eagle. Sometimes this story follows the second part of "Raven Burns a Girl's Groins." After Raven's son is born, the boy is stolen by Thunderbird. Raven carves a wooden whale. (The story of "Raven Kills Pitch" may be inserted here, and Raven then uses the pitch to complete the construction of the wooden whale.) Raven and his friends float in the artificial whale and are spotted by Thunderbird, who sends out his three sons, one at a time, to catch the whale. Each son is unable to lift the whale, either because there is a heavy rock in it, or because they become stuck to the pitch. Raven and his friends kill the thunderbirds, until only one is left.

Other variants of the tale have nothing to do with the abduction of Raven's son, but rather with the abduction of someone's wife. She may possess magic gifts, such as the ability to produce a bowl of berries that is never empty, no matter how many are consumed. Thunderbird desires her, and manages to abduct her. (In one Kwakiutl version, she is abducted and rescued three times; in another Kwakiutl version, she is only abducted once, but there are three attempts to rescue her.) The husband is told to transform himself into a fish, and he lets himself be caught in Thunderbird's weir. When the woman brings the fish into the house, it tells her to save the bones and put them back into the sea. The fish is eaten, and the woman puts the bones into a bowl and wades out into the sea. Thunderbird tells her not to go too far, but she wades further and puts the bones into the water. The bones become a fish again, and the fish carries her off. When he gets home, he and his friends try to think of a way to avenge themselves on Thunderbird. At that point they make the artificial whale, and the story continues as above.

The story appears among the Kwakiutl, Heiltsuk, Nootka, Oweekeno, and Comox but not further north (Boas [1916] 1970, 711–16; Boas 1932, 14–16).

31 The Arrow of the Supernatural Being

Once Kotsiku, Panther [i.e., Cougar], went into the mountains to hunt goats. He had his bow and arrow ready to fire in his hand, when he met the mountain spirit Toalatlitl. This person asked, "Whose bow and arrow are you carrying there?" Kotsiku answered, "They belong to Toalatlitl." He was glad because of this and exchanged weapons with Kotsiku. Since that time Panther has hunted mountain goats with ease. He entertained all the animals, except that to Raven he gave nothing. So this one decided to go and hunt mountain goats by himself. He also met Toalatlitl, who asked him, while pointing at Raven's weapons, "Who owns this bow and arrow?" Raven answered, "Who else but Raven?" Then Toalatlitl became angry and abandoned

Raven. So it happened that he killed no goats. But he was ashamed to come home with empty hands. Therefore he cut open his own chest, took some fat out, put it into the quiver that he carried on his back, and went back home. He now boasted that he had caught many mountain goats, and gave his sisters his own fat, which he had caused to increase considerably. They took the fat and laid it on the fire. Then Raven cried, "Oh, don't put the fat on the fire, it hurts me." When they didn't listen to him, he became ill. His intestines rumbled and he nearly died. But Kotsiku only gave food to Raven's sisters, and nothing to Raven. At that Raven became angry and said to Kotsiku, "Don't you know that the people want to kill you? You had better flee from here and not let yourself ever be seen again." Kotsiku took Raven's advice. Then the sisters became angry, because their brother had robbed them of their breadwinner. (Boas 1895, 245–46)

This is the Bella Coola version of the story, but the Tsimshian version is quite similar. In a Nootka version, Raven torments a hungry small bird by refusing to share herring with it. The small bird goes moose hunting, and wolves take the place of the mountain spirit. When the wolves ask the small bird who killed the moose, he says that he found it dead. The wolves help the bird carry the moose home. Raven attempts to duplicate the small bird's feat, but when the wolves ask him the question, he says that he alone killed the moose. When he finally struggles home with the meat, he leaves it outside the house for a while, but when he goes out again to get it, it has been turned into rotten wood.

The story is also found among the Halkomelem and Chilcotin, and the same basic tale (without Raven) appears among the Nez Perce and Ojibwa. The core of the tale is that the second character claims that the weapons or the skill belongs to himself alone, and thereby fails to show humility towards the deities (Boas [1916] 1970, 716–18).

Button blanket with raven design (Haida). *Photograph courtesy of the Royal British Columbia Museum, Victoria, British Columbia, CPN1413.*

3

RAVEN TALES
IN EASTERN ASIA

EASTERN SIBERIAN TALES BEAR A STRONG resemblance to those of the Northwest Coast. Bogoras wrote:

The mythology and folklore of northeastern Asia are essentially different from the Uralo-Altaic mythology, and point to a group of conceptions and a mode of expression which have little relationship to those of the interior of Siberia; on the contrary, they possess affinities eastward along the shores of Bering sea to the northwestern part of America. The differences of both mythological cycles are so distinct and important that one may almost assume that, from an ethnographical point of view, the line dividing Asia from America lies far southwestward of Bering strait, extending from the lower part of Kolyma river to Gishiga bay [i.e., due south]. In the whole country east of this line, American ideas, or, more properly speaking, ideas characteristic of the North Pacific coast of America, prevail. . . . The folklore of the Ainu . . . must be classed within the same group of ideas. (Bogoras 1902, 579–80)

However, some Raven tales—or, at least, tales which were often incorporated into the Raven cycle—extend far west of Bogoras' line. "The Deluge" is widespread in the Old World, and one explanation for the raven's change of color, "The Painting of the Birds," seems to be found in Southeast Asia. "The Bungling Host," complete with Raven, is apparently found in Lapland, as well as south of the Amur River, among the Orochi—although perhaps the Orochi may be included with the Ainu as "east" of Bogoras' line.

In this chapter, we shall be looking not at all the major Siberian Raven tales, but at Siberian tales that resemble the major North American ones. Approximately half of the major North American tales have Siberian counterparts. Looking at the proportion from the opposite point of view is less easy, because of the relative scarcity of Siberian material (in particular, there are not always enough data to determine whether a tale is major or minor), but one could say, for example, that between a third and a half of the Koryak tales in which Raven is a principal character have North American counterparts (Jochelson 1908, 354–63). Exactly how much correspondence there is between North American and Siberian tales, however, depends on one's criteria for determining correspondence. In the tales we shall be looking at, often the only point of similarity is the presence of a somewhat widespread folktale motif; Jochelson and Bogoras are even more liberal in their analyses than I shall be.

There are some subtle but important differences between the Chukchi raven figure and that of the Koryak:

(1) Among the Chukchi, two important figures are Kurkil (Raven) and Creator. They are regarded as two separate characters. Kurkil, however, is involved in the theft of the sun, and he may be responsible for the creation of rivers and humans, although at other times Creator is said to be responsible. Kurkil is more of a transformer than a creator.

(2) The tales of Kurkil make up only a small proportion of Chukchi tales.

(3) Among the Koryak, two important figures are Big-Raven and Raven-Man. Big-Raven is a god, he is very often referred to as "Creator" (although sometimes distinguished from the Supreme Being), and he is distinct from Raven-Man, who is more of a rascal, a trickster, although Big-Raven himself often plays a trickster role.

(4) The tales of Big-Raven (with his wife Miti, his son Ememqut,

his daughter Yinea-neut, other members of the family, and his would-be son-in-law Raven-Man) make up a large proportion of Koryak tales.

Jochelson claims that "almost the entire Koryak-Kamchadal mythology is devoted exclusively to tales about Big-Raven" (1908, 355). Chowning says that Jochelson's remark is "quite misleading," and that "the stories . . . more often concern his wholly human son [Ememqut] than Big-Raven himself" (1962, 2). Chowning may be exaggerating herself, in the opposite direction: the tales in which Big-Raven plays the dominant role are about equal in number to those in which his son Ememqut plays the dominant role.

Jochelson explains the two figures, Big-Raven and Raven-Man, among the Koryak, vs. the single raven figure Kurkil among the Chukchi, as follows: "Big-Raven and Raven-Man of the Koryak are merged into one person named Kurkil (Raven); and the Creator of the Koryak myths, identified by the Koryak with Big-Raven, appears among the Chukchee . . . as being independent of Kurkil, but the same as the Supreme Being. From this we may draw the conclusion that the raven of the Chukchee . . . has lost its place as the ancestor of the tribe . . ." (Jochelson 1908, 342). The important word is "merged." Again, Chowning disagrees. "It seems more likely that a single Raven was split by the Koryak, who were further removed from American influence than the Chukchee, than that the Koryak situation was the original one. The Koryak merged the transformer with a vague creator to produce a clearly defined high god, while stories in which Raven was bird-like made for the postulation of a separate Raven-Man . . ." (Chowning 1962, 2). For Chowning, the important word is "split."

We shall return to the question of whether Raven was or was not originally a creator in the final chapter. What is more important at the moment is simply to note that the Koryak have two Ravens, one a creator and one a trickster. Whether the process was one of "splitting" or "merging" is another issue.

We might get a better idea of the flavor of the Siberian tales by first looking at one that Bogoras calls "the most widely known of the

Raven tales peculiar to the west coast of Bering sea." The following is his summary of the Kamchadale version.

The Raven puts on his raven-breeches and raven-boots and goes strolling on the beach, where some small mice have found a little seal. They try to conceal it. When unable to do so, they pretend that it is a log, though it has eyes, eyelashes, claws, etc. The Raven is not deceived. He kicks them aside and carries away the seal. In the night-time they come to his house, led by the smallest of them, *axgike* ("hairless" in Koryak), eat up all the cooked meat, and defecate into the dish. Besides, they put some sharp stones in the boots of Raven and of his wife. In the morning, after their tricks are discovered, the Raven again puts on his raven-breeches, takes his raven war-club, and starts to seek revenge; but the Mice call him their grandfather, and give him a large cake of berries mixed with fish. Then they offer to louse him. After lulling him to sleep they sew to his eyebrows some strips of red fur. When he awakes he sees everything around as if on fire, hastens home, calls Miti, and requests her to sacrifice the worst of their sons in order to appease the flames. The next morning the Mice again lull the Raven to sleep and sew a bladder-bag on his buttocks, so that he defecates into the bladder and cannot find his excrements, but afterward is frightened by the rattling noise they produce behind his back. After that he sets out to catch partridges, but, instead of bringing the birds home, he eats them all when visiting the snares. The half-starved Miti finally discovers that his hunting cabin in the forest is full of partridges. She catches one, plucks it alive and sends it to the Raven's cabin, instructing it to frighten him by crowing and by beating its wings. The Raven is so badly frightened that he flies home, followed by the plucked partridge, which repeats every cry he makes. Miti kills the bird-charm and sits down before the window to mend her coat. [The mice, driving by in sledges, block the light. Miti thinks it is her nose blocking the light, so she cuts it off, then cuts off her lips and cheeks for the same reason.] At last Miti discovers that the mice are the real cause of her trouble. Then she brings out a large bag, and, putting it across the trail of the Mice, catches them all and hangs the bag on a high larch-tree, intending to preserve them for the coming winter. (Bogoras 1902, 647)

The following are east-Asian tales that have North American counterparts. In some cases, the similarity is quite strong, while in other cases the resemblance consists only of a few shared motifs, or of a general idea.

ORIGIN TALES

1 The Earth Diver; The Deluge

Vogul

An old man and his wife live alone in a house that is entirely surrounded by water. They have a white raven. One day, after a loud noise, a diver (i.e., loon) appears from the sky and dives to the depths of the water. After several attempts, and after nearly running out of breath, it rises with a piece of earth on its beak. The next day another waterfowl arrives and does the same thing. The man and woman send the raven out to see how large the earth has become. The raven returns in one hour, since the earth is still quite small. The next day they send it out again, and it returns at noon. It does not return from its third journey until evening, and this time it has become completely black. The couple ask the raven what has happened, and it replies that it has fed on a human corpse. They curse the bird and tell it that it will not be able to kill animals in the woods or fish in the water, but that it must appear when humans have killed animals, and that it must often go to sleep hungry (Dähnhardt [1907–12] 1970, 1: 63–64).

Samoyed and Yakut

In a Samoyed tale, seven people are saved in a boat during the Deluge. After seven days, a diver (loon) manages to bring up a piece of turf, and the people ask God to create a new earth from it. In a similar Yakut version of this story, the devil performs the same service as the diver (Holmberg 1964, 313–14, 322).

Altai

Up to the time when the flood (jaik) hid all the earth, Tengys (Sea) was lord over the earth. During his rule there lived a man called Nama, a good man, whom Ulgen commanded to build an ark (kerep). Nama, who had three sons, Sozun-uul, Sar-uul, and Balyks, was already failing of sight and therefore left the building of the ark to his sons. When the ark, which was built on a mountain, was completed, Nama told his sons to hang from its corners and walls eight cables of eighty fathoms each, by the help of which he could later determine "how many days it takes for the water to rise eighty fathoms." After this had been done, Nama entered the ark, taking with him his family and the various animals and birds which, threatened by the rising waters, gathered around him. Seven days later the cables attached to the earth gave way and the ark drifted free. This showed that the water had already risen eighty fathoms. When seven days had elapsed again, Nama told his eldest son to open the window of the ark and to look around. Sozun-uul looked in all directions and then said: "Everything has sunk under the waters, only the summits of the mountains are in sight." Later, when ordered by his father to look out again, he was able to answer: "Nothing is to be seen, only the sky and the waters." At last the ark stopped on eight closely situated mountains. Then Nama himself opened the window and set free the raven, which, however, did not return. On the second day he released the crow, and on the third the rook, but neither of these returned. On the fourth day he sent out the dove, which returned with a twig of birch in its beak. From this bird Nama also heard why the other birds had not returned. The raven had found the carcase of a deer, the crow that of a dog, and the rook that of a horse, which they had stayed behind to devour. Hearing this, Nama became enraged and laid a curse on these birds, saying: "What they are doing now, let them continue with to the end of the world!" (Holmberg 1964, 364–65)

3 The Theft of the Sun

Chukchi versions of "The Theft of the Sun" are similar to those of the Northwest Coast, although the impregnation of the sun-keeper's daughter may be missing. The Chukchi tales, however, sometimes include "The Wall of Dawn," which appears in North America only among the Bella Coola. The only Koryak tale that resembles "The Theft of the Sun" is one in which roles are both multiplied and reversed: Raven-Man swallows the sun, and the daughter of Big-Raven must tickle Raven-Man to get him to release it.

According to Bogoras, "the American incident of the leaf swallowed by the chief's daughter, who afterward gives birth to a child who is no other than Raven, is repeated in some Chukchee versions. The Raven, in the course of a contest of strength in supernatural power with a mighty shaman, transforms himself into a leaf of *Polygonum polymorphum* (in another versions into a hair), and drops into a pool. A girl carries him to her house in a bucket, but he is found out by his rival" (Bogoras 1902, 645).

Chukchi

In a Chukchi tale, a man loses his reindeer herd but finds a woman in a snowbank. They marry and produce a boy and a girl, who in turn marry and produce more children. Nephews marry their aunts, and so on, until a tribe is created. The tribe moves west.

> But the earth had no rivers at all, and moreover, it was dark. There was no sun, there were no stars. They moved on and found a wolf. He had a large reindeer herd. After a while they found a raven and then a wagtail. They stopped here and one man said, "It is strange. Why is it always so dark? We cannot keep proper watch upon our herd. Oh Wagtail, please make some light." The wagtail said, "I shall find the raven Kurkil and take counsel with him." He found Kurkil who at that time was as white as snow. He said to Kurkil, "How shall the people live? What is a world without any light in it?" Kurkil said, "Very well, let us go and see what can be done." They went and found the ptarmigan. His name was Kaggeelin (the Coughing One). All of them said, "Let us make some light in the world." The snow-bunting, Notarmin by name, (Ground-Creeper) said, "let us visit the land of the dawn." They pecked hard on both sides of the dawn, and even

broke their beaks. The raven, however, made them sharp again, but the beaks were now quite small. The raven pecked at the dawn and pierced it. So the dawn came in. The raven said, "Now let us go for the sun." He flew straight upward. He came to the world above. A little girl was playing ball there with something round. He said, "Throw it over to me." She answered, "I will not." But after a while she threw it to him. Raven caught it in the air and threw it far off. It became the sun. Then he took another ball from the girl and threw it upward. It became the other luminary, the moon, the second lamp. He took a third ball and kicked it upward. It stuck to the moon, and the moon increased and became full. So the moon is created of two balls. The girl was playing with another ball. The raven took this and threw it upward. The ball shattered to small pieces and they became stars. Then he also kicked the girl upward, and she stuck to the moon and remained there. In the meantime his clothes were burned by the fire of the luminaries and became black. (Bogoras 1928, 301–02)

In other Chukchi versions, Raven tells the girl to ask her parents for the balls. They are reluctant, and when she gets the balls, Raven catches them and flies off (Bogoras 1928, 303–04). In North American tales, it is the reborn raven who asks for the balls, but Bogoras notes that in the Chukchi tales "the Raven and the small girl clamoring for balls never appear as the same person" (1902, 645).

With regard to "The Wall of Dawn," Bogoras notes: "The Raven gathers (in other versions creates) various birds. They fly off toward the dawn and try to pierce the stone wall of the day with their beaks. The partridge breaks a part of hers, and therefore has a very short beak now. The Wagtail is so worn out by fatigue that his body shrinks, and he begins to shake as he does now. At last, one of the three birds (Raven in one version, Wagtail in another) succeeds in making a small hole, and the dawn passes through" (1902, 640).

Koryak

The most important "sun" story among the Koryak begins with a rivalry between Raven-Man and Little-Bird-Man for Yinea-neut, the daughter of Big-Raven. Little-Bird-Man wins her hand by stopping a snowstorm. Out of jealousy, Raven-Man swallows the sun.

Little-Bird-Man (Piciqalanl) and Raven-Man (Valvamtilan) came to Big-Raven (Quikinnaqu) to woo his daughter. Said Miti, "I prefer Raven-Man." Big-Raven said, "I prefer Little-Bird-Man." While they were discussing the merits of the visitors, a violent snowstorm broke out. Big-Raven said, "Whoever shall put an end to the snowstorm shall marry my daughter." Raven-Man said, "Prepare some travelling-provisions for me, and make a few pairs of boots. I intend to go far away." No sooner had Raven-Man gone out than he dug a hole in the snow behind the dwelling, and ate his provisions. When he had eaten all, he returned into the dwelling, and said, "I have been unable to stop the snowstorm: the sky is all broken."—"Enough! I see that you are not the one who can accomplish this task."—"I will try," said Little-Bird-Man. "Well," said, Big-Raven, "we will prepare provisions for your journey." But Little-Bird-Man replied, "I do not want anything. Just give me a pail-cover, a shovel, and reindeer guts." They gave him everything he asked for, and he flew up to the sky, right to the spot where it was pierced. He tried to cover the hole with the lid of the bucket, but it was too small. Little-Bird-Man put the guts around the cover and stopped up the hole temporarily. Then he returned to Big-Raven. "The cover is too small," he said. "There is a crack left, through which the wind may still blow, though not so violently as before." They gave him a large lid, and again he started off to the sky. He flew up, changed the lid, pushed the guts around the rim, and covered it over with snow, which he piled on with his shovel. Then he flew back to Big-Raven.

The storm had stopped completely. "Well," said Big-Raven, "I will give you reindeer to go to your people." But Little-Bird-Man replied, "We do not need any reindeer: we will walk." Off they went. When they came to a river, Little-Bird-Man said to his wife, "Sit down on my back, I will carry you across." She replied, "You are too small, I shall crush you."—"No," he responded, "I can easily carry you across, you will not crush me." As soon as Yinea-neut sat upon Little-Bird-Man, he was completely crushed, and lay there dead. Yinea-neut put her husband's body upon the palm of her hand, and sat down under the shade of a stone-pine tree. She sat there for a long time. At last she began to cry, and said, "I shall die of starvation, my husband is dead." Suddenly she heard a voice behind, saying, "Why are you crying? Here I am, your husband." She turned back, and beheld a young, powerful man. Near by there was also a tent, and a herd of reindeer were in the pasture. The reindeer had silver antlers and silver hoofs. She said to the man, "You are lying. Here is my husband, he is dead." He answered, however, "This is only the shape that I assumed in order to serve your father for your sake. Now you see me in my true shape. Here are my relatives too. I purposely let myself be killed, that I might appear in my true shape, and to bring my reindeer over here." She trusted him, and followed him into his tent. Everything in the tent was made of iron,—posts, sledges, and snow-shoes. Soon she gave birth to a son named Self-created (Tomwoget), who had iron teeth, which, when he laughed, emitted sparks.

Once Little-Bird-Man said to his wife, "I want to drive you over to your father. Your parents, no doubt, think, 'Our daughter left our house on foot, and we do not know whether she is alive or not.' Let them see how you are getting along." They prepared plenty of meat-paste for the journey, extracted an ample supply of marrow from bones, and got ready to go. When they reached Big-Raven's house, the people shouted from inside, "Little-Bird-Man is coming!" and they came out to meet them. They were conducted down into the dwelling. There they staid for some time, played, and had a very jolly time.

Suddenly it grew dark. Raven-Man had swallowed the sun. It grew so dark that the women could not go out for water. Nevertheless, the two sisters, Yinea-neut and Canai-naut, managed to bring some water. They groped their way to the river as though they were blind, and drew some water. A young man came up to them unexpectedly, and said to Canai-naut, "give me your pail: I will carry the water for you." The girl did not wish to give it to him, and said, "I will carry it myself." But he insisted, and carried her pail into the house. They asked the girl, "Where has this man come from?" The women said, "We did not want to let him carry our water, but he took our buckets by main force. He wooed Canai-naut, and married her." His name was River-Man (Veyemilan).

"I am a shaman," he said, "and I want to discover who causes the darkness." They gave him the drum, and, after he had tried his skill, he declared, "I see! it is Raven-Man, who has swallowed the sun."

Yinea-neut said, "I will go to him, and set the sun free." She put on her reindeer-leather coat and went to Raven. She found Raven-Man lying in his house. He did not get up, and remained silent so as not to open his mouth. Yinea-neut approached him, and said slyly, "I have left Little-Bird-Man. I have a longing for you." She embraced him firmly, and tickled him under his arm. He laughed, and opened his mouth. Then the sun escaped, and it became light again. Yinea-neut said to Raven-Man, "Have you no fork?" He gave her a raven's beak. "Well," she said, "I am your wife now. Let us go to my father's house."

They started off. She said to him, "Go ahead, and I will follow you." He went ahead. Then she stabbed him with the raven-beak from behind, and killed him. Raven-Man's sister, Raven-Woman (Velvem-neut or Vesvem-neut), was yearning for her brother. She went to see him, and found him lying dead outside. She cut off his beak, and went back crying. Her mother asked, "Why are you crying!"—"Yinea-neut has killed my brother," said she, and threw to her the beak that she had cut off. It struck her mother's eye, so that the old Raven-Woman died.

Yinea-neut came home in the mean time, and told how she had set the sun free, and killed Raven. "Now, we shall always have light," said she. Meanwhile, the young Raven-Woman came, and Yinea-neut gave her dried fish to eat.

Big-Raven said to Little-Bird-Man, "Now you may go to your folks." Big-Raven gave reindeer and well-loaded sledges to Yinea-neut. Later on River-Man and Canai-naut also drove off. Ememqut went with them and married River-Man's sister, River-Woman (Vayam-naut). Ememqut returned with his wife to his father's. She bore him a daughter, who was called Ice-Hole-Woman (Aime-neut). Thus they lived together with Big-Raven. (Jochelson 1908, 250–53, 378)

Ainu

An Ainu tale from Japan resembles "The Theft of the Sun," particularly the Koryak version.

When God created the world, the evil one did all he could to frustrate His designs, especially with regard to human beings. Now, after all things were made, the evil one perceived that men could not possibly live without the light and warmth-giving sun. He, therefore, made up his mind to destroy that beautiful and useful work of creation, and thereby injure men. So he got up early one morning, long before the sun had risen, with the intention of swallowing it. But God knew of his designs, and made a crow circumvent them. When the sun was rising, the evil one came along and opened his mouth to swallow it; but the crow, who was lying in wait, flew down his throat, and so saved the sun. (Batchelor n.d., 270)

5 The Theft of Fresh Water

Chukchi

Then [Raven] said, "I will create water." So he flew over the earth, dragging one of his wings behind him. He traced one furrow after another with it, and water streamed down along these furrows. Thus he created rivers and also the sea, making fit places for fishing and for spearing the seal. He created fish, walrus, whale and thong-seal. Then he created Bear, Wolf, Red-Fox and Arctic-fox. After that he said, "Enough of gifts. Now I will become invisible. I will soar above the earth and cause fright with clattering." And so he became the thunder. (Bogoras 1928, 305)

A second Chukchi version includes the "urine" motif that we saw in some Northwest Coast versions: "Raven flies and defecates. Every piece of excrement falls upon water, grows quickly, and becomes land. . . . He began to pass water. Where one drop falls, it becomes a lake: where a jet falls, it becomes a river" (Bogoras 1910, 152).

Koryak

Big-Raven (Kutqinnaqu) walked along the seashore, and found a Crab (Avvi), who was sleeping on the shore. "Crab, get up!"—"No, I shall sleep until the water comes and takes me back to my house!"— "Get up! I am hungry." Meanwhile the water rose. "Now, mount on my back," said Crab. "I will take you to my place, and give you some dried meat of the white-whale, seasoned with blubber." He took

Big-Raven to his village, and said to his fellows, "Bring some white-whale-meat! Let us feed our guest!" At the same time he added under his breath, "But give him nothing to drink. Conceal the river, and empty all the vessels and water- buckets."

They had supper and went to sleep. About midnight Big-Raven awoke. "Oh!" said he, "I am very thirsty;" but nobody answered. "Halloo! I am thirsty!" but still all kept their peace. Big-Raven jumped up, and hurried to the water-buckets; but there was no water in them. He ran to the river, and found only dry stones. "Oh!" said he, "how very thirsty I am!" then he came back, lay down on his bed, and sang, "My elder daughter, Yinea- neut, is drinking her fill, and I am without a drop of water. I am afraid I am going to die. If someone would give me a drink, I would give him my daughter." But Crab whispered, "Keep your peace; do not answer until he offers his other daughter."

After a while Big-Raven sang again, "Oh! I am indeed very thirsty! If anybody gives me to drink, I will give him my daughter Anarukca-naut."—"Now," said Crab, "give him to drink." They gave him water, and with one draught he emptied the bucket. "This is not enough," said he. "I shall go to the river." He went to the river, and drank it dry. "Now," said he, "carry me back to my village."

They took him to his house; and he said to his daughters, "Do not be angry with me, O my daughters! I have promised to give away both of you." Ememqut married one; and White-Whale-Man (Sisisan), the other. Big-Raven vomited the water, and created rivers out of it. (Jochelson 1908, 311–12, 372)

A Kamchadale story is very similar, except that Raven has to give away three daughters instead of two (Jochelson 1908, 334–35). In another Kamchadale version, Raven simply steals the water (Bogoras 1902, 644–45).

8 War with the South Wind

Another episode of the Raven myth, widely known on the west coast of Bering sea, is his struggle with the giants who produce the cold wind. Bad weather causes famine in a village. The Raven wants to stop the tempest. He starts for the land of the Wind-giants. His sledge is an old boat, and for sledge-dogs he selects from among the wild beasts

Raven silkscreen by Bill Reid, 1972 (Haida). *Photograph courtesy of the Royal British Columbia Museum, Victoria, British Columbia, CPN14643.*

two white foxes (in another version, two white hares). He finds the Wind-giants shovelling snow with the shoulder-blades of a whale. The Raven cheats them out of all their meat and peltries, and even induces them to throw into his boat their fur coats and caps. Then he makes good his escape, regardless of their frenzied cries, and leaves them to be frozen to death. (Bogoras 1902, 649)

In one of the rare cases in which the Chukchi Supreme Being makes an appearance, we are told of how Raven put an end to excessive rain:

> At one time rain was pouring down continually. All of Big-Raven's belongings got wet. . . . Finally he said to his eldest son, Ememqut, "Universe (Naiminen) must be doing something up there." . . .
>
> They went out, put on their raven coats, and flew up. They came to Universe. While still outside, they heard the sound of a drum. They entered the house, and found Universe beating the drum, and his wife Rain-Woman (Ilena) sitting next to him. In order to produce rain, he cut off his wife's vulva, and hung it to the drum; then he cut off his penis and beat with it, instead of an ordinary drum-stick. When he beat the drum, the water squirted out of the vulva, which caused rain on earth.
>
> . . . Big-Raven and Ememqut pretended to leave the house . . . but they both turned into reindeer-hair, and lay down on the floor. . . .
>
> Big-Raven said to his son, "I will make them fall asleep." . . . Big-Raven took the drum and stick, and roasted them over the fire until they were dry and crisp. . . . They arose, and Universe began to beat the drum; but, the more he beat it, the finer the weather became. (Jochelson 1908, 142–43)

Jochelson adds: "The tale is told in order to put a stop to a rain or a snow storm and is not supposed to be told in good weather."

9 The Theft of Fire

Chukchi

The Creator drops some seal-bones . . . and they become the first man and woman. . . Finally the Creator himself goes and finds the human couple. They are naked and half-witted, and stand or lie motionless on the ground. He starts to teach them how to eat and to drink, how to carve with the knife, and even how to defecate. Finally he orders them to lie down, covers them with a skin blanket, and teaches them how to copulate. Then he brings reindeer, makes a fire-drill and gets fire from it. He instructs the reindeer-people to be nomads, and the dwellers of the sea- coast to hunt the seal. Finally the fire-drill is forgotten on a camping-place, and transforms itself, of its own volition, into a Russian. (Bogoras 1902, 641)

"Then the Raven gets fire, using his forefinger as a fire-drill, and his foot as a base for the fire-drill. Another time he strikes one thumb-nail against the other, like flint and steel." (Bogoras 1902, 642)

According to Jochelson, the Koryak also believe that Big-Raven gave the fire-drill to mankind (1908, 22).

10 The Origin of Humans

Chukchi

There are several Siberian accounts of the creation of humans, usually rather brief and confused. In one Chukchi version, Raven sees his wife developing into a human form. Her abdomen enlarges, and that same night she gives birth to twin human boys, who laugh at Raven for his form. He flies away and discovers some men in tents. They tell him they are the product of the friction of sky and earth. But all Raven's children are males. Spider-Woman descends on a thread. She becomes pregnant and gives birth to four daughters. A man and a woman start living together, but they do not yet know about sexual intercourse, so Raven has intercourse with the woman, and she teaches the man how to do it. And so the human race multiplies (Bogoras 1910, 151–54). The tale confuses two or three tales of the origin of humans.

11 The Painting of the Birds

Siberian Eskimo

Believe it or not, but in olden times the raven and the owl were both white as snow.

One day they met in the tundra, and the raven said:

"Aren't you tired of being so white, owl? I know I am. Why don't we each paint the other a different colour?"

"All right," the owl replied. "We can try and see what comes of it, I suppose."

The raven was pleased.

"Good!" he cried. "Let us begin."

And he added:

"You paint me and then I'll paint you."

"Oh no," said the owl. "It was your idea, so it's you that has to paint me first."

"Very well," the raven agreed.

He scraped some of the burnt-out fat from a lamp, and, using that and a large feather plucked out from his own tail, set to painting the owl. He took great care doing it and drew grey spots of every size on each feather, larger ones on the owl's wings and smaller ones on her breast and back.

"Oh, how beautiful I've made you, owl!" cried he when he had finished. "Just look at yourself."

The owl looked at herself and could not get her fill of looking.

"Yes, indeed!" she said at last, pleased. "These spots are lovely. And now let me do the same for you. By the time I get through with you you'll be so handsome you won't know your own self."

The raven turned his head toward the sun, squinted his eyes and stood still. He was very eager for the owl to make a good job of painting him.

The owl set about it with great zeal. It took her some time and when she had finished painting the raven, she looked him over. Then, glancing from him to herself, she found that the raven was now brighter than ever and more beautiful than she. Angered that this should be so, she came up close to him, poured what was left of the fat she had been using over him and flew away.

The raven rubbed his eyes, and, seeing that he was now quite black all over, cried:

"Oh, what have you done! You have made me blacker than soot, darker than night!"

That is the end of my tale, and from that day on never has a raven been seen that was not black. (Zheleznova [1976] 1989, 46–47)

Malaya

Skeat gives us a Malay story that seems to be a version of "The Painting of the Birds":

The Argus-pheasant and the Crow in the days of King Solomon were bosom friends, and could never do enough to show their mutual friendship. One day, however, the argus-pheasant, who was then dressed rather dowdily, suggested that his friend the crow should show his skill with the brush by decorating his (the argus-pheasant's) feathers. To this the crow agreed, on condition, however, that the arrangement should be mutual. The argus-pheasant agreed to this, and the crow forthwith set to work, and so surpassed himself that the argus-pheasant became, as it now is, one of the most beautiful birds in the world. When the crow's task was done, however, the argus-pheasant refused to fulfil his own part of the bargain, excusing himself on the plea that the day of judgment was too near at hand. Hence a fierce quarrel ensued, at the end of which the argus-pheasant upset the ink-bottle over the crow, and thus rendered him coal-black. Hence the crow and the argus-pheasant are enemies to this day.

Skeat adds: "I believe that a similar story exists in Siam, the Siamese, however, making turpentine play the part of the ink in the Malay story" ([1900] 1967, 130–31).

Vietnam

"The Painting of the Birds" also seems to occur in Vietnam:

The raven and the pagoda cock were once men in the service of the

Holy One (Confucius), who transformed them to animals to punish them for their disobedience. To escape their punishment and to make the Holy One laugh, the raven covered himself completely with ink. The pagoda cock would have done likewise, but he had only enough black ink for half his body, so he took red ink for the other half. So now the raven is black, the pagoda cock half red and half black. (Dähnhardt [1907–12] 1970, 3: 67)

A second Vietnamese version is more similar to the North American tale:

The peacock and the raven once lived in harmony on a small plantation. They painted each other for amusement. At this time neither the peacock nor the raven had his present appearance. The peacock was rather plain and wanted to take the raven's place as the most beautiful animal in creation, so he painted the raven completely black. (Dähnhardt [1907–12] 1970, 3: 373)

13 The Origin of Salmon

Koryak

It was at the time when Big-Raven (Quikinnaqu) and his people lived. They had nothing to eat: so Big-Raven went down to the sea. Finding Fish-Woman (Emem-neut) there, he took her home. She spawned, and the people ate the spawn. After a while Big-Raven married Fish-Woman. Miti grew angry; and one day, when Big-Raven had gone out, Miti struck Fish-Woman, and killed her. Then she cooked her meat. Some of it she ate herself; the other part she left for her husband. Big-Raven came home, and called out, "Fish-Woman, come out!" Then the one who had been cooked not long before came out of the storeroom. She placed some food before him, and said, "Miti has killed me and cooked my flesh."

Next morning Big-Raven again went away from his house. Miti immediately caught Fish-Woman, and struck her on the head with a club. "Now," she thought, "I have killed her!" But when Big-Raven came back, she came to life again, and gave him food, as before. After that Fish-Woman went away, saying, "If I stay here, Miti will surely make an end of me." Big-Raven came home, but she was gone. He went to the sea, and called, "Fish-Woman, come here!" She answered, "No, I will not come. Miti will kill me again." She did not come back. (Jochelson 1908, 292, 378)

In another Koryak story, Big-Raven's daughter Yinea-neut and niece Kilu go on a trip. Kilu playfully throws a fish bone at Yinea-neut, which sticks to her face and makes her turn into a kamak (spirit). She falls asleep, but is woken up by Fish-Man, who marries her. They catch many fish. They go to visit Big-Raven, but Kilu is jealous of her cousin, so she asks Big-Raven's other daughter to strike her with a fish bone so that she too can become a spirit. Her wishes are granted, and she also marries Fish-Man. They all live together, catch many fish, and have many children (Jochelson 1908, 296–97).

TRICKSTER TALES

15 The Killing of Grizzly Bear

There are no Siberian tales that closely resemble the North American tale of "The Killing of Grizzly Bear," but Bogoras mentions a Chukchi tale in which a bear is killed in a manner similar to that in which Raven kills Grizzly Bear's wife. A fox and a bear are arguing about what is the most terrifying thing in the world. The fox says it is humans, but the bear sarcastically says that partridges are worse. The bear tries to kill a man, but the man wounds him with a spear. "At his next meeting with the Fox, he is ashamed to acknowledge his defeat, and says that his belly is aching. The Fox offers to cure him, and makes him swallow hot stones, which scald his intestines. Then she feeds her children on his body" (Bogoras 1902, 655).

16 Cormorant's Tongue Is Torn Out

Chukchi

The wolf, who owns a reindeer herd, insults the raven by saying that it eats excrement and has no reindeer. The raven retaliates by taking the sun, moon, and stars away. The wolf offers his two sisters to the raven, if he will bring back the light. The raven consents. The girls ask the raven to show him his tongue. He does so, and they tie it with a thread. Raven sleeps with both girls, but the next morning, when he goes home to his wife, he cannot untie his tongue, and so he loses the ability to speak.

In another Chukchi tale, the tongue of Raven's daughter is tied up with a thread by her sister-in-law (Bogoras 1928, 302–03). In a Koryak tale, Seal ties the tongue of Raven's daughter so that she cannot tell her father how she is being mistreated (Jochelson 1908, 152–54).

18 Raven's Beak Is Torn Off

No tale of Raven's beak being torn off appears in Siberia, but in one Koryak tale, Big-Raven is so hungry that he eats Fox-Man's ladder and lamp. Fox-Man baits a hook with some meat, and Big-Raven gets his beak caught on the hook. He struggles until the line breaks, and he flies off with the hook in his jaw (Jochelson 1908, 317–18, 371).

19 Raven Is Swallowed by a Whale

Kamchadale

Raven (Kutq) walked along the sand-pit, and found a small seal. He said, "If you were a good find, you would not be so far from the water;" and he pushed it back into the sea with his toe. Then he walked on, and found a spotted-seal. "If you were a good catch, you would not lie so far from the water." After that he found a big ground-seal, and treated it in the same manner. Then he did the same with a white-whale, and with an old bowhead-whale. At last he found a finback-whale, and then he said, "This is a good thing." He shouted to the people of the village, "I have found a whale!" Then the Koryak reindeer- breeders were seen to be hurrying to the whale from various directions. They had large knives. Raven was so frightened that he jumped into the mouth of the whale-carcass. He found there plenty of oil, and, filling his mouth with it, he jumped out and flew away. A Fox woman saw him and asked, "From where are you?"—Yum, yum," replied Raven [trying to speak: "yunyun" means "whale"]. "What did you say?"—"From the whale!" As soon as he said so, the oil dropped down from his mouth, and fell on the Fox's back. "That is good," said the Fox. "I also have received some oil." She wrung her coat dry, and filled a large wooden trough with oil. Raven also stored the remaining oil. Then the Fox made a cake of all kinds of berries, and sent it to Raven to show her gratitude, and by way of payment. With it, however, she killed him. (Jochelson 1908, 339-40, 368)

20 Raven Travels with His Slave

In the third part of the North American story of Raven and his slave, Raven pretends to be dead, so that he will be left with the provisions. In a Koryak tale, Big-Raven runs out of food, so he hitches some mice to a sledge and goes to visit the Reindeer people, who give him food and other supplies. When he gets back to his family, he makes his nose bleed and then says he is dying. He asks to be buried in an empty underground house, and he wants to have various kinds of food placed around him. But his son discovers him making a meal. Big-Raven's wife Miti cuts off her breasts and attaches them to a partridge, which flies into the underground house and scares Big-Raven, so that he runs out (Jochelson 1908, 224, 375).

22 Raven Becomes a Woman

Koryak

Big-Raven (Quikinnaqu) said, "Let me transform myself into a woman." He cut off his penis and made a needle-case of it; from his testicles he fashioned a thimble; and from the scrotum, a work-bag. He went to a Chukchee camp, and lived there for some time, refusing, however, all the young people who offered to take him for a wife. Then Miti ran short of food. She dressed herself like a man, and tied a knife to her hip. From her stone maul she made a penis. She came to the Chukchee camp, driving a reindeer-team, and remained there to serve for Big-Raven's marriage-price. She proved to be so nimble and active that very soon she was given the bride. They lay down together. "Now how shall we act?" asked Miti of Big-Raven. He answered, "I do not know." After a while his penis and testicles returned to their proper places, and he was transformed into his former state. Then he could play the husband, and said to Miti, "Let us do it as we did before." In the morning they exchanged clothes and went home. (Jochelson 1908, 323, 366; cf. 193–96)

23 The Bungling Host

Orochi

The story of "The Bungling Host" is found north of Japan, among the Orochi:

> A Crow once came to pay an Otter a visit. The Otter made the Crow welcome, and, wanting to treat her guest to the best she had in the house, filled a large pot with water and hung it over a fire. As soon as the water was warm the Otter dived into it, and the Crow stood there and stared at the pot in wonder, for she could not understand where her hostess had gone to.
>
> All of a sudden up came the Otter out of the water, and not alone, either, but with a pike in tow. She left the fish in the pot and herself jumped out of it and sat down beside the Crow.
>
> When the pike was all cooked and ready to eat, the Otter offered it to her guest, and she and the Crow had a grand feast.
>
> On the next day, not to be outdone, the Crow, in her turn, invited the Otter to come and see her. As soon as the Otter arrived, the Crow filled a pot with water and hung it over a fire. The water boiled up, and the Crow, deciding to do as the Otter had done, jumped into the pot and was boiled alive!
>
> And thus ended the friendship of the Otter and the Crow. (Zheleznova [1976] 1989, 40)

The story also seems to occur much further west, in Lapland:

Once upon a time, Crow and Seal kept house together; they took turns going to the barn to make their food. When the seal made the food there was fat in the pot, and when the crow made the food, there was no fat in the pot. At one time the crow went and peeked to see how the seal did it. Then he saw that the seal cut his chest and warmed his chest by the fire and let the fat drip into the pot. The crow said, "I'll do that, too." The next time the crow started to make the food, he cut his chest and warmed it by the fire and burned to death. (Qvigstad 1927, 3: 45)

Another Lapp version is as follows:

Once upon a time the seal and the raven started to cook fish. The raven wondered where he would get the fat for the fish. The seal said, "That's easy. I am going to get fat." The seal warmed his chest and the fat dripped on the fish. The raven began also to try and warm his chest. His chest became burned and there was no fat from it, so the seal got the cooked fish, and the raven ate the fish raw. (Qvigstad 1927, 3: 45–46)

30 War with the Thunderbird

There are no Siberian stories that duplicate the plot of "The War with the Thunderbird," but two or three Koryak stories have a wooden whale. There are also stories of fish and reindeer made of wood (Jochelson 1908, 232, 286, 370, 379).

Once Big-Raven (Quikinnaqu) said to his wife, "Let us take our daughters to the wilderness; let them live there." Then they took their daughters, Yinea-neut and Canai-naut, into the wilderness. They settled down by themselves in an underground house. Their father and mother would eat fat reindeer-meat, but to their daughters they would send the lean pieces.

Yinea-neut and Canai-naut became angry with their parents. They fetched a large log, made a whale out of it, and put it into a pail of water. On the following morning they looked into the pail, and saw that the whale had grown so large that there was no room for it inside. They carried it to a small lake. On the following morning they saw that there was no room for it in the lake. They transferred it to a larger lake; but on the next day the whale had grown so large that there was not room enough for it in the large lake. They put it into a river, entered it, and said, "Spotted-Whale, take us over where there is a settlement." Thus they were carried to sea. (Jochelson 1908, 232, 370)

In a completely different Koryak story with a wooden whale, a small kala (evil spirit) feels hungry. In spite of his mother's warning, he goes to Big-Raven's house to steal food, but he gets caught in a snare. Big-Raven asks him if he would like to be made into a cover for the roof-hole. The kala says no. Big-Raven asks him if he would like to be a plug for the vent-hole, or a work-bag, and again the kala says no. So Big-Raven asks him if he would like to be a leather harpoon line, and the kala says yes. Big-Raven turns him into leather and cuts him into a harpoon line, which he spreads outside. The people of Frost-Man come to steal the line, but the line shouts to Raven that he is being stolen. Then the people living down the coast come to steal the line, and the line shouts, but fails to awaken anybody, and so it is stolen. Big-Raven's son Ememqut makes a wooden whale and goes down the coast until he reaches the village. The coast people throw a harpoon, which catches in the side of the whale. Ememqut whispers to the line, "Why are you biting me? I have come to take you home." He throws raspberries into the water, and the coast people go after these instead of the whale. So Ememqut manages to go home with the line, which Big-Raven thereafter keeps inside the house (Jochelson 1908, 285–86).

31 The Arrow of the Supernatural Being

In a Nootka version of "The Arrow of the Supernatural Being," Raven and a little bird are competitors in their dealings with beings who have power over game. Raven acts foolishly, while the small bird acts wisely. In two versions of a Koryak tale, Raven-Man and Little-Bird-Man compete for the hand of the daughter of Big-Raven. Raven-Man is foolish and obnoxious, and Little-Bird-Man acts wisely and gallantly, and therefore marries the woman. One version includes Raven-Man's swallowing of the sun; in the other version, he becomes intoxicated with fly-agaric mushrooms, knocks his head on a post, and splits his skull. His brain drops out, and he thinks it is a pudding, and so he eats it (Jochelson 1908, 143–44, 250–53, 372).

Chilkat blanket depicting ravens with fish (Tlingit). *Photograph courtesy of the Royal British Columbia Museum, Victoria, British Columbia, CPN18464.*

4
THE FORMS OF THE TALES

IT IS SOMETIMES SUGGESTED THAT THE RAVEN tales of North America fall into two somewhat overlapping categories: origin tales, mythological tales, or creator tales, and secondly, trickster tales. Raven's role as a creator blends into his roles as a transformer (one who changes the landscape and living creatures into their present forms) and as a culture-hero (one who is responsible for cultural innovations, such as the use of fire). As Radin says,

> the cycle connected with [Raven] consists of two parts, the first recording incidents dealing with the creation of the world and of natural phenomena, the second, those relating to Raven's insatiable hunger and how he, by force and trickery, obtains or tries to obtain all he wants. . . . In the first part of the cycle the incidents are relatively well integrated, in the second no specific order need be followed. (1956, 156)

Absolute definitions are impracticable, since no Raven tale would fit perfectly into any category. Yet a few generalizations are possible. The origin tales have a number of common features. In the first place, though they rarely deal with the very beginning of the universe (this is true of North American myths in general), they do involve certain major events of "early times": the placing of the sun in the sky; the origins of rivers, lakes, mountains, and the tides; and the creation of humans and animals. Other incidents, more related to human culture, might also be placed in this first category, such as "The Theft of Fire." An explanatory element, regarding the question of "why the raven (or crow) is black," is sometimes added to one of these tales.

Secondly, the origin tales are the most widespread. These tales occur in large parts of North America and Siberia, and similar tales are found in other parts of the Old World.

And thirdly, there is a difference in the way the two kinds of tales are treated by Northwest Coast narrators. Among the Tlingit, "The Earth Diver" (or "The Deluge") and "The Theft of the Sun" are told when raising a totem pole for a dead chief or a member of his family, while the less mythological tales can be told on any occasion (Swanton 1909, 374). Franz Boas felt that "no order can be brought into the northern Raven tradition," ([1916] 1970, 571) but then added an enlightening footnote:

> I have recently had an opportunity to discuss this matter with Mr. [Louis] Shotridge, an educated Indian from Chilkat. He claims that among the Tlingit the Raven legend, so far as it refers to the Creation, follows a regular sequence. Upon closer inquiry, he said that everything had to be created in definite order,—daylight before the world became inhabitable; water before fish could be produced; and so on. In answer to my question regarding the order of the other incidents of the tale, he claimed that they were only told to offset the serious parts of the tale, in order to entertain the listeners, and that there was no particular order in which these were told. (Boas [1916] 1970, 582)

The above passage actually seems to be saying three things:

(1) The tales fall into two categories, "origin" tales and other, less serious tales.

(2) There was a fixed sequence to the telling of origin tales (the English word "order" is ambiguous; it can mean "sequence," or it can have the looser meaning of "pattern").

(3) The origin tales were reserved for special, formal—one might

say, religious—occasions, while the remaining tales were quite the opposite.

There is little other evidence for a fixed sequence to the origin tales, although it is often implicit in the plots: Raven cannot threaten to let out the sun over the fishermen, for example, until he has stolen the sun. But there is ample evidence for the other two points, that the tales form a dichotomy and that they differ in seriousness. What are referred to as "the other incidents of the tale," or rather the second group of tales, the non-mythological or, as most scholars now categorize them, "trickster" tales, also have a number of common features, largely derogatory. Raven appears as a liar, a cheat, and a fool, and his accomplishments are usually a matter of accident. Raven, however, is not the only trickster. The term is applied to other North American characters, such as Coyote, Blue Jay, Old Man, and Manabhozo (Hare).

The roles of creator and trickster are not incompatible. It may be difficult for those of us with a Christian heritage to conceive of someone who could both create the world (or at least put it in order) and be a target of ridicule, but the common feature is Raven's personality. He is selfish and greedy; he is always active, sometimes too active for his own good; he is inquisitive and clever, though sometimes not clever enough; he is like a child or an animal—in fact, he is like a raven. He represents "the beginnings of things." Unlike the Christian God, Raven is not omnipotent, omniscient, or benevolent. But we shall be examining the relationship of creator and trickster in more detail in chapter 7.

Like the characters of other primitive cultures, Raven can take both human and animal form, although the distinction between the two is usually unclear and, in terms of the particular story, apparently unimportant. According to various Northwest Coast tales, humans were created first, and some of them later took certain animal forms. Other tales simply suggest that the difference between humans and animals was not as clear-cut as it now is. In Eskimo tales, humans and animals are usually distinguished from each other (even if the animals talk), but where they blend, the combination can be rather mechanical: "It is believed that in ancient times all animals had the power to change their forms at will. When they wished to become people they merely pushed up the muzzle or beak in front of the head and changed at once into man-like beings" (Nelson 1899, 425). The Australian Dreamtime resembles the Northwest Coast mythical past in several respects, but partly by the fact that again the human-animal dichotomy is blurred.

On the Northwest Coast and in easternmost Siberia, the raven appears not only as a figure of myth, but also in various other aspects of native culture. There is controversial evidence hinting that the raven was a totemistic (ancestral) figure and, in general, a figure of religious veneration.

The first possibly totemistic aspect to consider is the fact that the raven is part of the social structure of the Tlingit and other cultures. The Tlingit have two moieties or phratries (subdivisions), called Raven and Wolf (or sometimes Raven and Eagle), while the Haida moieties are Raven and Eagle. Some Eskimo and Athapaskan tribes also have a Raven moiety: the Tahltan moieties are Raven and Wolf (Teit 1919, 207), for example, and so are those of the Tanana (McKennan 1959, 124), while the Eyak moieties are Raven and Eagle (Birket-Smith and De Laguna 1938, 123). Francis Poole claimed that the Haida used to cover themselves with black paint as a sign of their descent from "crows" (ravens?):

My rifle being still loaded, I emptied it on the way back, and brought down a splendid specimen of the native crow (*corvus caurinus*), called *klail-kula-kulla* by the Indians. The Queen Charlotte Indians hold views, on the subject, decidedly in advance of the Darwinian theory; for their descent from the crows is quite gravely affirmed and steadfastly maintained. Hence they never will kill one, and are always annoyed, not to say angry, should we whites, driven to desperation by the crow-nests on every side of us, attempt to destroy them. This idea likewise accounts for the coats of black paint with which young and old in all those tribes constantly besmear themselves. The crow-like colour affectionately reminds the Indians of their reputed forefathers, and thus preserves the national tradition. (Poole [1872] 1972, 136)

A second hint of totemism may be seen in beliefs regarding the killing of ravens. The Buryat of Siberia believe that anyone who kills a raven will soon die (Armstrong 1958, 74). Among the Tlingit, it is prohibited or considered unlucky to kill a raven (Krause [1885] 1956, 125). The Bering Strait Eskimo say that "to kill a raven will cause the Raven Father to become very angry and to send bad weather . . ." (Nelson 1899, 426). Similar beliefs are found in many other parts of North America, though most cultures regard the mythical Raven and the actual bird as independent figures.

Further evidence for a religious aspect to Raven may be seen in the fact that when the Tlingit saw the ships of the explorer La Pérouse, they thought they saw Raven returning (reminiscent of the Aztecs, who thought Cortez was their god Quetzalcoatl), and they were afraid that if they looked at him they would be turned to stone (De Laguna 1972, 1: 259).

One often finds a vaguely defined Supreme Being in North American and Siberian myths. He is often identified with the sun, the sky, the "above," but he is also identified with animal and human figures. The creator god may stand below this Supreme Being, as for example, among the Koryak (Jochelson 1908, 23–24). Some of the Chukchi describe Raven as the companion of the creator, although other Chukchi say Raven is the "outer garment" of the creator; the Koryak and the Alaskan Eskimo often regard the creator and Raven as identical, although some of the Koryak say the creator only becomes a raven when he puts on his "raven coat" (Bogoras 1902, 640; Jochelson 1908, 17, 142, 149; Nelson 1899, 425). Raven is said to have founded shamanism, and sacrifices were once made to Big-Raven in Siberia. A religious aspect can rarely be seen in other North American or Siberian animal figures; the circumboreal bear cult is probably the closest parallel. Some of the zoomorphic gods of the western Old World may also offer a few clues to the original status of Raven.

THE BIRTH OF RAVEN

The tale of Raven's birth incorporates two principal motifs, that of the jealous uncle and that of the deluge or earth diver.

> It seems plausible . . . that the opening of the Raven . . . tales is essentially a deluge myth which has been elaborated in different directions, but presents in all these tales the beginning of the present world. . . . Among the Tlingit the elaboration of this incident [of the deluge] is based on the jealous-uncle story. Among the Tsimshian the true deluge story remains apart from the Raven story; and we recognize the deluge idea only in the general setting of the beginning of the tale. The Haida form is a mixture of the Tlingit and Tsimshian forms. (Boas [1916] 1970, 641)

Boas rarely speculates on the data he so assiduously compiles, but he is willing to theorize somewhat on the meaning of "The Birth of Raven":

> It would seem . . . that the essential idea contained in all the versions is the acquisition of supernatural power by Raven. In the Tlingit and Haida stories this power is manifested in the boy's contest with his uncle. In the Tsimshian version it is acquired by his heavenly birth. The latter form accounts also, in a way, for the boy's refusal to eat. As a heavenly boy he needs no human food; and when he is endowed with human qualities by eating scabs, the transformation is overdone, and, instead of eating like an ordinary human being, he becomes voracious. ([1916] 1970, 640)

The great diversity in the form of "The Birth of Raven" recalls Stith Thompson's remark about European folktales: "The place where a folktale is most likely to suffer change is in its introduction, where a preliminary action really proper to another story but capable of being logically joined to the one in question is easily substituted" (Thompson 1977, 28).

The story ends with Raven's voraciousness and expulsion. As to why it should be the consumption of scabs that leads to Raven's voraciousness, I can only assume that the storyteller is choosing something that is as close as possible to no food at all and yet can still be considered food. The fact that the scabs sometimes come from his own body reinforces that concept, since one is hardly eating well if one is eating oneself. Perhaps the story can be interpreted to mean: At first Raven has no need for food, but when he consumes the smallest possible amount of food, his appetite becomes monstrous, and he eats an entire village's food supply. Or, by extension, the transformation from heavenly creature to earthly creature is complete.

THE EARTH DIVER AND THE DELUGE

Anna Rooth has carefully studied the many New World and Old World stories of a great flood that covered the earth, but particularly those in which a raven is involved. In her book-length study of these tales (1962), she presents a large number of examples, and shows that they form themselves into two great clusters, each derived from one of two original tales. The first is an extremely ancient tale, that of "The Earth Diver," and the second is a similar Judeo-Christian (Semitic) one, that of Noah and "The Deluge."

The two tales probably had a common origin, involving the creation of the earth from the depths of the sea by an animal figure. They then split into two stories and remained separate for many long centuries before intermingling again, as they do in North America.

"The Earth Diver" is the most common creation myth of North America and Siberia. The entire world is originally covered with water. The creator says that he can make dry land if an animal can dive to the bottom and bring back some mud. Several animals try and fail, but finally one of them returns, exhausted but successful. In Siberia it is usually the loon (also known as the diver) who succeeds, while in North America it is usually the muskrat, although the loon makes an appearance in Ojibwa versions (Blackwood 1929, 326, 329), and of course in the Tlingit story. In many versions, the earth grows larger every day, and an animal is sent out to see how much it has grown.

"The Earth Diver" is very popular in North America, but it is equally popular in the Old World. It is found all over northern Asia, in much of Europe, throughout India, and in Ceylon, Burma, the Malayan peninsula, Borneo, Indonesia, the Philippines, and the Gilbert Islands. Holmberg believes the story began in India (1964, 328–30; cf. Hatt 1949, 28–36).

"The Deluge," which is Semitic in origin, can be seen in Genesis, although this is a fairly late form of the tale. God decides to punish mankind for its wickedness by sending a great flood from above and below the earth, but he tells Noah to build an ark and save his family and two of each kind of animal (or seven—the number alternates throughout Genesis 6 and 7). The water rises and falls, killing all other people and animals. Finally the water subsides, and the ark lands on the mountains of Ararat. Noah sends out a raven ("which went to and fro, until the waters were dried up from off the earth"). Then he sends out a dove, which returns from its second expedition with an olive leaf, indicating that the earth is beginning to dry.

The raven appears in the deluge story as early as the seventh century B.C., in the Assyrian version of the *Epic of Gilgamesh*, although "The Deluge" without the raven is known from much older Near Eastern literature.

Although "The Deluge" evolved into a Judeo-Christian story, it was never entirely a Biblical one, because many of the details of the story are not found in the Bible. Some of the details were popular beliefs that developed during the Middle Ages, when most people had little access to the Bible. Other details originated from earlier Semitic forms but are not found in Genesis.

The most important non-Biblical addition to the deluge tale, for our purposes, is that by the Middle Ages the raven was commonly said to have been turned from white to black as a punishment for a crime: he had failed to return to the ark, and/or he had chosen to stay and eat the corpses of drowned people and animals. This crime and punishment are found in Jewish, Christian, and Islamic tradition.

The consumption of corpses is particularly relevant to the Jewish conception of clean and unclean animals.

When North American Indian tales describe this punishment of the raven or crow, they are following the Judeo-Christian deluge tradition, not that of the native earth diver, which originally contained no such incident.

The raven's role in "The Deluge," like many of his other mythical roles, has its origin partly in real life: it was common at one time for mariners to send out birds from ships in order to find land. Pliny records that the merchants of Taprobane (Sri Lanka) sent birds out from their ships and followed their routes in order to find land (*Natural History* 6.22.83). Jason and the Argonauts, according to Apollonius Rhodius, sent a dove ahead of their ship in order to test the feasibility of sailing between the Clashing Rocks (2.326–579). When the two heroes of Aristophanes' *Birds* leave Athens for the land of birds, they are guided by a jackdaw and a crow. The *Mahabharata* mentions sending out doves from ships in order to find land (Rooth 1962, 158).

The *Landnamabok* says that Floki decided to sail west from Norway (A.D. 846) to test the report that there was a large island beyond the Faroes. He dedicated three ravens to the gods. When he was out of sight of land, he let loose one raven. It circled and returned to the Faroes. Later he released the second, which circled several times and returned to the ship. The third, however, headed northwest. Floki followed and reached the coast of an island that he named Iceland.

Christian storytellers had apparently lost sight of this tradition when they described the fact that Noah's raven did not return as a failure, instead of the very sign Noah was looking for. But during the Middle Ages the raven was seen in Europe largely as a figure of evil, and so the misinterpretation was inevitable.

"The Earth Diver" and "The Deluge" are common tales in much of North America, though neither is clearly defined on the Northwest Coast. As we have seen, both tales are often simply woven into "The Birth of Raven." But the "flood" stories of the Northwest

Coast are probably derived largely from the Judeo-Christian deluge tale. One obviously Semitic version among the Tlingit is a rather confused tale in which Raven's uncle kills his sister's children to prevent the spread of mankind; it is also said that he punishes them for some sort of misbehavior. He sends a flood, but some people save themselves by fastening their boats to the tops of mountains (Krause [1885] 1956, 177).

"The Deluge" may be unusually ancient among Judeo-Christian influences in North America. Most European and Near Eastern folktales to reach the New World did so, via the Atlantic, in post-Columbian times. But the fact that "The Deluge" was so widespread in North America in early historical times suggests that it reached the New World, via Siberia, before Columbus.

Whether the raven was originally part of the separate earth diver tale is hard to say; I suspect not, since there are many Siberian and North American versions of "The Earth Diver" without the raven. The earth diver myth and the raven figure were both well known in Asia and North America, and so it may be that the two were occasionally placed together, with "The Deluge" and its own raven providing a model for doing so.

THE THEFT OF THE SUN

The most popular Raven tale is "The Theft of the Sun." According to Jennifer Gould, the significance of the story is that "it marks a turning point in the history of the order of the universe" (n.d., 67).

Before that event, the world was in darkness; afterwards, there was light. According to the Tlingit (in Swanton's version), Raven then went to the banks of the Nass river, where he saw people fishing. They were making a lot of noise, and Raven threatened to let out the daylight over them if they did not stop. (Or he asked them to take him across a creek.) They refused to comply, so he released the daylight, and all the people ran off into the woods or the water, becoming the type of animals whose skins they wore. Those who had been wearing seal skins became seals, those who had been wearing marten skins became martens, and so on.

Gould notes that in the Tsimshian versions, the people fishing are either ghosts who then disappear or perish, or frogs who are driven away and who then turn into stone.

She also notes that the Haida do not seem to regard the story of Raven and the sun as quite so important. They substitute the moon for the sun, but the significant difference is that there is no description of the fishermen being turned into the various animals; for the Haida the greatest early event is Raven's creation of land from two pebbles.

Regarding the Tlingit and Tsimshian versions of "The Theft of the Sun," she concludes:

> . . . The event of liberating daylight marks the end of chaos, formlessness, and lack of reciprocity. In the above accounts, formlessness is indicated by darkness, by animals that change back and forth into human beings, and by animals (people) that can be heard but not seen. Chaos is indicated by the noise and quarreling that angers Raven as well as by formlessness. Lack of reciprocity is indicated by the chief who hoards the sun, and the animal people who both refuse Raven's gift and refuse to help him. In these senses, the origin of daylight marks the beginning of order and in particular, social order. (n.d., 71)

Outside the area of the Tlingit, Tsimshian, and Haida, further variations occur in its form.

One is that the episode of the impregnation of the sun-keeper's daughter is absent south of the Chilcotin, and also in parts of Alaska, while in Siberia it is often absent from Chukchi tales, and completely absent from Koryak tales. There is a Koryak tale in which Earth-Maker turns into a piece of reindeer-marrow, and Raven's daughter becomes pregnant after eating it (Jochelson 1908, 300), but Jochelson may be wrong in suggesting that this story is derived from "Raven Steals the Sun," since the motif of conception by eating is found in several New World and Old World tales that usually have nothing to do with Raven. In Irish myth, the raven-god Lug transforms himself into an insect and falls into the cup of Deirdre, so that he may be reborn as the hero Cuchulain (Krappe 1936, 242). However, the motif of transforming oneself into a small object, being swallowed, and being reborn occurs even in an Egyptian papyrus of about 1250 B.C. (Thompson 1977, 275).

The second change has to do with "The Wall of Dawn." The Bella Coola version of "The Theft of the Sun" is composed of three stories or episodes. It begins with "The Wall of Dawn," found nowhere else in North America. Then there follows the story of "The Painting of the Birds." The account concludes with the usual "Theft of the Sun." The connections among the three episodes are not very clear.

The puzzling elements in the Bella Coola story can perhaps be illuminated by comparing it to the Chukchi version. In the Bella Coola story, we are told that Raven got the deities to tear the curtain, and it is said that the sun "did not shine clearly and brightly, but only through a thick fog." Then, after the painting episode, we are given a slightly different account of the situation: "Raven, however, was not satisfied with the sun, which shined so dimly, and decided to look for another." Why should one sun be hidden behind a curtain, and the other be hidden in a box in a house? What happens to the first sun after the second is liberated? In the two Chukchi versions of "The Wall of Dawn" that Bogoras presents, the wording suggests that the dawn and the sun are regarded as two separate things, to be created separately: "The raven pecked at the dawn and pierced it. So the dawn came in. The raven said, 'Now let us go for the sun.'"

The Chukchi version gives us an explanation of the relationship between dawn and sun, but it is conceivable that both the Chukchi and the Bella Coola combined two sun stories that were originally separate.

By looking at the Chukchi story, we can also guess why the Bella Coola inserted "The Painting of the Birds." According to the Chukchi story, in the process of piercing the wall of dawn, the wagtail, the ptarmigan, and the snow-bunting acquire their present shapes, by pecking too hard or by working too hard. The explanatory element has a causal relationship to the piercing of the wall. In the Bella Coola tale, on the other hand, the birds also acquire certain of their present characteristics, but no causal relationship is stated.

The simplest explanation for the difference between the Chukchi tale and the Bella Coola tale is that the former is closer to the original form.

There are two versions of a Chukchi tale in which Hare takes the place of Raven: he goes to the sun-owner's house and kicks the sun ball out of the house (Boas [1916] 1970, 648; Bogoras 1910, 155). Two common North American stories are "The Man Who Acted as the Sun" and "The Sun Snarer" (Thompson 1977, 314), but these are not related to "The Theft of the Sun." In California it is Coyote who creates the world and steals the sun, although the Coyote tale resembles Raven's "Theft of Fire" rather than Raven's "Theft of the Sun":

Eagle was the first man here, he was the chief. . . . Coyote came up to visit Eagle at his home. . . . Coyote had lots of supernatural power. "Nephew, I came here to tell you that the animals have been playing all the time out there in one place."

The animals who were playing kept the sun hidden somewhere inside. Chicken Hawk and Wild Goose were among those animals. Now those people had the sun hung on a hook in a house. They had fire too. . . .

Coyote said, "I will be a cut-down green log in the woodpile. When the wood is burned out they will come and get me and put me on the fire. I will be green and therefore will not burn." . . .

When they [i.e., Eagle and Coyote] reached the place where the people were they found they had two fires and were playing the pitching-poles game. Coyote had a long elder-wood pole for Eagle. When Coyote, as a log, was on the fire Eagle was to pitch his pole into the two fires and scatter them, while Coyote, being near the sun, was to reach up and grab it.

Then Coyote changed himself into a log and someone came out to get firewood. When Coyote was laid on the fire Eagle was ready. He pitched his pole into the fires, scattering them all over the place, then he rushed off. Coyote jerked down the sun and ran off after him. . . . The people were all on fire and were trying to put it out.

Slate totem pole depicting bear, raven, and beaver (Haida). *Photograph courtesy of the Royal British Columbia Museum, Victoria, British Columbia, CPN2869.*

Then they saw that the sun was missing. They all started in pursuit. By this time Eagle had reached home. . . . Coyote . . . got to Eagle's house safely. . . .

Then Eagle said . . . "I want you to go 'way off east with sun and hang it up there at Watsat'aocao pa'an nim (forked or jointed place: the horizon) where the world meets. This is the only place it can be, at any place else it will burn us. Don't put it any nearer." . . .

Coyote went off with the sun, but he got tired and hung it low down, not where it belonged. . . .

Eagle told him to go back and fix the sun properly. . . . Then [Coyote] rushed back and moved the sun up to the right place. . . . Coyote returned, and the two went into the house to talk over the improvements that the sun made. Coyote boasted of what a fine clever fellow he was. (Gayton and Newman 1940, 31–32, 60)

THE THEFT OF FRESH WATER

Teit has an interesting anecdote about Ganuk, the owner of the fresh water (who also appears in "The Origin of Fog"):

According to Tahltan information, this mythological personage appears to be a water-deity or sea-god of the Tlingit. He is said to have been the first man created (or the first man in the world). He is the most ancient of the ancients, and has been from the beginning of the world. He is the only man who ever lived that never told a lie. Among the Tahltan, when a person's word is doubted or certain information is in doubt, they say, "Kenuge [Ganuk] told me," or "Kenuge said it." This saying is much in vogue among young people, and is always meant in a jocular way. The Tlingit are said to pray to Kenuge, asking for fine, clear weather. They make offerings to him when supplicating, and they put their offerings or sacrifices in the fire or in the sea. When they pray to him, they turn seaward or to the west. (1919, 201–02 n.)

In some Northwest Coast versions it seems that the owner of the fresh water has caused a drought, and that the only place where one can find water is under the roots of alder trees—although this may have been a separate story. Perhaps the fact that certain kinds of alders grow in wet soil is of some relevance here: if one were searching for water in a drought, under the roots of alders might be a logical place to look.

In one of the Chukchi tales, after Raven creates rivers and the sea, he becomes the thunder. The Thunderbird is derived from both the raven and the eagle. He is commonly said to carry off whales in his claws, and Bogoras mentions another Chukchi tale, in which "the Raven, or Raven's son, assuming the form of the thunder-bird, carries away a whale in his claws, but is swallowed by the whale while he bends too low over its mouth. . . . In the folklore of the Chukchee the giant thunder-bird appears sometimes to be the same as the raven; but more frequently it is a kind of giant eagle of supernatural strength and power. . . . In other tales, the thunder-bird is called *ginon-gale,*—'middle (sea) bird,'—perhaps in relation to the albatross." (Bogoras 1902, 645, 663). Among the Ostyak, the Thunderbird is a "black, loudly screaming bird" (Holmberg 1964, 227).

It is interesting that in Kwakiutl and Nootka versions, Raven forms the rivers by urinating, because this is precisely how the Chukchi Raven does it, and how the Chukchi "Universe" creates rain. The "urine" motif is not entirely restricted to the Raven tales, since even in Aristophanes' *Clouds* we are presented with the facetious theory that rain is caused by Zeus's urinating through a sieve (ll. 373–74).

The tale of "The Theft of Fresh Water," though superficially similar, is quite distinct from "The Earth Diver" and "The Deluge." In the first place, it is fresh water, not the ocean, that is created, except in the Chukchi version mentioned above, in which Raven creates both rivers and the sea. And in spite of what would seem to be obvious opportunities, the tale is never combined with "The Earth Diver" or "The Deluge." As we shall see in chapter 5, it is "The Theft of Fresh Water" which bears a resemblance to the European belief that "crows indicate rain."

THE PAINTING OF THE BIRDS

Kleivan (1971) has compiled twenty-five Eskimo variants of "The Painting of the Birds." She uses the material for a rather complex "structural analysis" instead of simply examining the variants for their actual forms, but perhaps we can do so now. Her variants can be summarized as follows (I have reversed the order, so that the forms are presented in a roughly west-to-east sequence):

(1) Kaniagmiut. A man creeps up to a house full of birds, who are startled and have no time to dress. In the hurry, the raven is painted black all over, and the gull all white.

(2) Noatagmiut. The raven and the loon agree to paint each other so that they might hunt animals without being seen. The raven paints the loon. The loon paints the raven, then says that since the raven never dives, it should not be white, and paints him black all over, so that he will look like a rock.

(3) Nunatagmiut. The raven and the loon agree to paint each other with charcoal so that enemies cannot see them so easily. The raven paints the loon very nicely. The loon paints the raven, but the raven asks to be painted a little darker. The loon maliciously blackens him all over. The raven throws ashes at the loon, hitting him on the neck.

(4) Mackenzie Eskimo. The raven paints the loon. The loon begins to paint the raven with soot all over as a preliminary, but a man comes up behind them and frightens them, so the loon cannot finish the job.

(5) Mackenzie Eskimo. The raven and the loon paint each other to look more beautiful. The raven paints the loon with black spots and lines. The loon, as a preliminary, paints the raven black all over, but before he can continue, a man frightens them away.

(6) Copper Eskimo. The raven tattoos the loon, and asks to be tattooed in return. The loon doesn't want to, and throws soot on the raven.

(7) Copper Eskimo. The raven tattoos the loon, then asks the loon to paint it, but the loon throws lamp-black over it.

(8) Copper Eskimo. The gull steals the raven's food, and the raven is angry. The gull throws charcoal on the raven to blacken it, and likewise blackens the oldsquaw duck.

(9) Netsilirmiut. The raven tattoos the loon with a nice pattern, but then becomes impatient and throws ashes on the loon. The loon retaliates by throwing soot on the raven.

(10) Caribou Eskimo. The raven paints the loon, but the loon is not satisfied with its pattern, so it spits on the raven, turning it black. The raven hits the loon and cripples it.

(11) Iglulirmiut. The raven tattoos the loon. The loon tattoos the raven, who will not keep still. The loon throws dung on the raven and blackens it. The raven throws a fire stone at the loon and cripples it.

(12) Iglulirmiut. The raven and the loon tattoo each other. The raven tattoos the loon. The loon then tattoos the raven, but the raven is not pleased with the result, and will not keep still. The loon pours soot all over the raven. The raven throws fire stones at the loon and injures its thighs.

(13) Eskimo of the west coast of Hudson Bay (Iglulirmiut or Caribou Eskimo). The raven uses thread blackened with lamp-black to make speckles on the loon's dress. The loon uses the needle on the raven, who will not sit still. The loon pours the lamp contents over her. The raven breaks the loon's legs.

(14) Baffin Island Eskimo. The raven uses lamp soot to make spots on the owl. The owl decorates the raven's dress, but the raven will not keep still, so the owl pours lamp-oil over her.

(15) Baffin Island Eskimo. The raven makes a white and black dress for the owl. The owl makes a white dress for the raven. The raven will not keep still, so the owl pours lamp oil over him.

(16) Labrador Eskimo. The owl and the raven quarrel. The owl tips a lamp over the raven and blackens him with the soot. He is ashamed and cries "qaq! qaq!"

(17) Labrador Eskimo. A man paints his two children. He paints one (loon) with square spots. The loon is ashamed, and escapes to the water.

(18) Polar Eskimo. Two children use a dripping-bowl from a lamp to paint each other. A man startles them, and the whole contents of the bowl fall onto one of them. They become the falcon and the raven. The raven cries "qaq!"

(19) Polar Eskimo. The falcon and the raven are painting each other. They are startled by a man, so that the hawk spills soot all over the raven, and the raven spatters the falcon with spots.

(20) West Greenland Eskimo. The raven and the loon paint each other to look more beautiful. The raven paints the loon beautifully. The loon paints the raven like a ptarmigan. The raven is angry, so the loon rubs him all over with soot.

(21) West Greenland Eskimo. The raven and a sea bird paint each other to look more beautiful. The raven paints the other bird pretty colors, but then gives it black legs. In retaliation, it paints the raven all black.

(22) West Greenland Eskimo. The raven and the loon paint each other to look more beautiful. The raven paints the loon. The loon maliciously paints the raven all black with lamp soot.

(23) Southeast Greenland Eskimo. The raven and the loon paint each other to look more beautiful. The raven paints the loon nicely. The loon paints the raven in exactly the same manner. The raven says his pattern is ugly and becomes angry. The loon is annoyed at the raven's fussiness, and paints the raven black all over.

(24) East Greenland Eskimo. The raven and the loon paint each other to look more beautiful. The raven paints the loon with spots of black mire so that it is beautiful. The loon does the same to the raven, but puts a spot where there should not be one. The raven becomes so angry that it rubs itself all over with mire.

(25) East Greenland Eskimo. The raven and the loon paint each other to look more beautiful. The raven paints the loon with speckles, some close together, others further apart. The loon paints the raven with spots of equal size, equidistant from each other. The raven sees a few spots that are out of place, tries fixing them, and does this for so long that it makes itself all black. The raven cries "qaq! qaq!" ("a skin for a sleeping platform").

The loon appears in sixteen of the variants, but the owl appears on Baffin Island, and the falcon among the Polar Eskimo. The variants in which a human appears, startling the birds, and causing one to spill something on the raven, are found among the Kaniagmiut, Mackenzie Eskimo, and Polar Eskimo. In most cases, the birds paint each other in order to be more beautiful, although sometimes such a motive is only hinted at. Fourteen variants involve soot, lamp oil, ash, or charcoal. Tattooing occurs among the Copper Eskimo, Netsilirmiut, and Iglulik Eskimo; we can assume (partly on the basis of example 13) that soot is used in the tattooing. On the west coast of Hudson Bay and on Baffin Island, the second bird blackens the raven because the latter will not sit still or because he complains too much. In six widely scattered cases, the blackening is due to a largely unexplained maliciousness on the part of the second bird. In Labrador and East Greenland, the raven cries "qaq" after being blackened, and on the west coast of Hudson Bay and on Baffin Island, the raven injures the loon's legs. (Loons are primitive birds, with somewhat reptilian skeletons, and their legs are set too far back for them to walk easily.)

To the extent that these twenty-five forms are statistically valid, we can say that the dominant form of the tale is that the loon and the raven agree to paint each other, in order to make each other more beautiful, but the loon blackens the raven all over because the latter is too impatient (the "central" form) or because the loon is malicious (a widespread form). The material with which the raven is blackened is usually a substance related to fire: soot, ash, charcoal, or lamp oil. Of the more prominent variations, a "western" and "polar" form involves the startling of the birds by a human, and a "central" form involves the raven's injuring of the loon's legs.

WHY THE RAVEN (OR CROW) IS BLACK

There are quite a number of explanations for why the raven or crow is black. Sometimes these tend to form an independent tale, but usually they are an explanatory element affixed to other tales, some of which we have already examined. Among the tales to which this element is added are "The Deluge" and "The Earth Diver," "The Theft of Fresh Water," "The Bungling Host," "The Killing of Pitch," and "Raven Kills the Salmon."

As we have seen, several North American tales ascribe the crow's change of color to sins he commits after "The Deluge": his failure to return or his consumption of carrion. But this explanation is due to Semitic rather than native tradition.

Many peoples of the Northwest Coast and the Arctic ascribe the raven's transformation to the incident of "The Painting of the Birds."

Many other peoples claim the transformation involves either fire or the sun. The Pawnee, as we saw, claim that the crow was turned black by trying to obtain fire from the sun. The Cherokee also say that the crow was turned black by trying to obtain fire (though not from the sun). In a Chukchi tale, Raven is turned black by the fire of the sun, moon, and stars. The change of color is sometimes part of the Tlingit "Theft of Fresh Water," but Raven's actual transformation is by smoke while he is escaping. In "Raven Kills the Salmon," it is sometimes ash that darkens the crows. Even in "The Painting of the Birds," it is usually soot, ash, charcoal, or lamp oil that changes his color—in other words, a substance related to fire. So fire is one of the most common ingredients in many explanations of the crow's change of color, with sun—itself a form of fire—as an equally dominant ingredient.

"The Painting of the Birds" seems to reappear in the eastern Old World. Other Old World explanations for the raven's change of color are part of the tangled web of tales involving sun and fire, which resemble the Northwest Coast tales of "The Theft of the Sun" and "The Theft of Fire."

THE TRICKSTER

Most of the Raven trickster tales belong to a tale cycle in which Raven himself is a rather replaceable character. I should point out that while Boas lists forty-five principal Raven tales, the tales are "supposed to be so numerous that one person cannot know them all" (Krause [1885] 1956, 180). In fact, hundreds of incidental and isolated raven or crow tales can be found throughout North America.

Paul Radin gives an account of the Winnebago trickster cycle that can be summarized as follows:

(Episodes 1–3) Trickster decides to go on the warpath, but he breaks many rules. Although he is the tribal chief, he plans to lead the war party himself, although it is forbidden for a Winnebago chief to do so. He breaks another rule of war preparations by cohabiting with a woman. He gives a feast and breaks the rules of etiquette by being the first to leave. Then he arrogantly breaks his boat, his warbundle, and his arrows.

(4–5) He kills a buffalo and starts to skin it, but his two arms get into an argument over who owns it, and his left arm gets badly cut up.

(6–8) He sees a man who keeps four tiny children in a bladder. He persuades the man to let him borrow two of them, but he is told to feed them only once a month. Instead, he feeds them quite often and they die. The man returns and tries to kill Trickster. Trickster is frightened, and he runs over the whole earth until he reaches the ocean.

(9–10) He jumps in and swims around, then asks several fish where the shore is, but discovers he has been swimming along the shore all that time. He gets out of the water and decides he would like to eat some fish, so he boils some water, drinks it, and tells himself that he has had a good meal. The only fish he gets is a dead one, which he buries to eat later.

(11) Trickster wanders on and sees what looks like a man beside a lake, pointing with his arm. He asks the man repeatedly what he is looking at, but gets no answer, then realizes that he has been talking to a stump; he also realizes why he is called the Foolish One.

(11–13) He comes to another lake and sees many ducks. He offers to sing songs for them to dance to, if they will keep their eyes closed. They do so, and he wrings their necks, until one opens its eyes and warns the rest. But Trickster has killed several of them, and he puts them on a fire to roast. He tells his anus to guard them. Foxes come by and are at first alarmed by Trickster's flatulence, but soon they eat his ducks and put the bones back in the ashes. Trickster wakes up and realizes what has happened.

(14) He is angry at his anus for not guarding the meat properly, so he takes a burning piece of wood and burns his anus. Later he finds pieces of fat by the side of the road and eats them, until he realizes that they are pieces of his own intestines that are falling out because he has burned his anus.

(15–16) Later he lies down, but he sees his blanket floating in the sky. He realizes that the blanket is so high because his penis has become erect, so he puts his penis in a box and carries it on his back. He goes on and sees women swimming on the other side of a stream, so he sends his penis across and it enters the chief's daughter. No one can get the penis out of her until an old woman jabs it repeatedly with an awl.

(17–18) Trickster sees a turkey buzzard and asks to be taken for a ride, but the buzzard drops him into a hollow tree. He is stuck until some women come by. He calls to them, telling them that he is a fat raccoon. They chop a hole in the tree, remove their clothes, and use them to plug the hole. When they are gone, Trickster escapes.

(19–21) He meets a fox, a jay, and a second bird, and they travel together. They build a lodge for the winter but run out of food. Trickster decides to make a vulva out of an elk's liver and turn himself into a woman, and then he goes to a village and is married by the chief's son. He gives birth to three boys. The youngest child cries and will not be pacified until it is given four things it asks for: white clouds (snow), blue sky (blue grass), green leaves, and some roasting ears. One day the chief's wife teases Trickster, and when Trickster chases her the liver falls off, so they know who Trickster is.

(22) He goes back home to his real wife and stays for a long time. But he sees that his son is quite grown up, so he decides to start wandering again. He is tired of staying in one place.

(23–25) He hears a plant say, "He who chews me will defecate!" Trickster says that he alone will decide when he will defecate, and he eats it, but soon begins to break wind. After a while he has produced a great mound of dung. He climbs a tree but falls into the dung. He runs off, blinded, and keeps knocking into trees; he asks them what kind they are, and finally one says it is the basswood by the water. Trickster jumps in and washes himself.

(26–29) Trickster discovers some plums, after mistakenly diving after their reflections in a pond. He goes to a lodge where two racoon women live and offers to take care of their children while the women gather the plums, but when they are gone he kills the children and eats them. He gets a skunk to dig a tunnel, and when the women come back he disguises himself and tells the women that Trickster, the killer of their children, is in the tunnel. They enter the tunnel and he burns them to death.

(30–31) While he is cooking the two mother raccoons, he hears a squeaking sound from the rubbing branches of a tree. He is annoyed and tries to split the tree, but his arm gets caught. Some wolves come by, and he asks them not to eat his food, but they do. He finally gets angry enough to split the tree so he can fall down.

(32–33) He hears a sound like that of people dancing, but it is only flies inside an elk's skull. He envies them for the fun they are having and uses magic to enlarge the skull so that he can get his head inside, but then he cannot get his head out. A woman comes by, and he tells her that he is a spirit, and that if someone will strike him on the head, he will give them powerful medicine, and in that way he is freed.

(34–35) Trickster sees a hawk and turns himself into a dead deer. The hawk tries to feed on the deer, which is still rather tough, by inserting his head in the deer's anus. Trickster jumps up and runs off. A bear sees Trickster and admires his tail (the hawk), so Trickster releases the hawk, then offers to prepare the bear for his new tail. He cuts out bear's anus, killing him, then boils him for food.

(36–37) A mink comes by, and Trickster suggests a race on the ice, with the loser to dish out food for the other. Trickster comes to a crack in the ice, and the mink shows him how to make the crack widen magically. Trickster falls in, and mink eats all the food.

(38–39) He wanders on, and he hears a chipmunk making fun of the penis Trickster still carries on his back. The chipmunk runs into a hole in a tree, and Trickster uses his penis to probe the tree, but his penis breaks off. He kicks open the tree, sees the pieces of his penis, and throws them away. They turn into plants of various sorts, but his penis is now a normal size.

(40) He meets a coyote and challenges him to a smelling contest. Trickster can actually smell nothing, but he notices in which direction the coyote is looking and heads there to find a village. He remarries and has a child and makes that place his permanent home.

(41–44) The next four episodes are versions of "The Bungling Host." Muskrat turns ice into lily-of-the-lake roots, snipe calls fish out of the water, woodpecker knocks on a pole to get a bear, and pole-cat breaks wind to kill deer, but Trickster is unable to imitate them.

(45) He sees the mink and feeds him fish oil, then sends him to the chief's daughter. The mink spends the night with her, but in the early morning the oil makes him defecate and he is disgraced.

(46) Trickster makes a horse fall asleep, then tells a mouse to go and tell the coyote that there is a dead horse to be eaten. The coyote arrives, and the mouse ties the coyote's tale to the horse so that it can be pulled to one side. The horse wakes up and gallops off, dragging the coyote along.

(47–49) Trickster's mischief is over. He goes down the Mississippi, removing obstacles in its bed that might annoy the people who will later live there. He moves a waterfall to a better place. He has his last meal on earth. His seat, kettle, dish, and the imprint of his buttocks can still be seen in the rock there, near where the Missouri enters the Mississippi. He leaves the earth, and he is now in charge of the world underneath.

The Winnebago trickster is known simply by that name: "The Winnebago word for trickster is *wakdjunkkaga*, which means *the tricky one*. The corresponding term for him in Ponca is *ishtinike*, in the kindred Osage, *itsike* and in the Dakota-Sioux, *ikto-mi*. The meaning of the Ponca and Osage words is unknown, that of the Dakota is *spider*" (Radin 1956, 132). The Winnebago Trickster is also called Older Brother, First-Born, the Foolish One, and occasionally (like the Crow and Blackfoot character) Old Man.

Yet the Winnebago have other mythical characters who sometimes take on roles similar to that of the trickster, or who have adventures that are the same as those undergone by the trickster. The Winnebago are not alone in sharing the trickster role with other characters. In fact, "among practically all the tribes where myths with Hare as a hero are found, he plays the double role of culture-hero and trickster. The exploits and incidents assigned among the Winnebago to both Trickster and Hare are, in these other tribes, credited to Hare alone. This two-fold function of benefactor and buffoon ... is the outstanding characteristic of the overwhelming majority of trickster heroes wherever they are encountered in aboriginal America" (Radin 1956, 124).

If I interpret him correctly, Radin sees the Trickster stories as, in part, illustrating the development of Trickster into a socially responsible being, with the trickster serving as a metaphor for humans; the trickster breaks, tests, and ultimately validates the social rules. As the tales progress, Trickster grows up, becomes civilized, and gains a realistic perspective on his place in relation to other beings.

The first four episodes of the Winnebago trickster cycle present a blatant travesty of the rules of war preparations. "Wakdjungkaga is to be desocialized, to be represented as breaking all his ties with man and society" (1956, 133).

In the next incidents, the trickster shows an utter disregard for many other rules of Winnebago society. "No ethical values exist for him. . . . He is still living in his unconscious" (1956, 133). From one episode to another, the trickster changes, but the process is a long one, and he has many stages to pass through. He begins as a being so primitive that he lacks self-consciousness.

His first real lesson is a lesson in fear (episodes 6–8). After carelessly allowing the two children to die, Trickster is nearly killed by the angry father. "He is not only isolated from man and society but—temporarily at least—from the world of nature and from the universe as well. Small wonder, then, that he is described as thoroughly frightened . . ." (1956, 134).

With later episodes, "the emphasis is now upon defining him more precisely, psychically and physically. . . . But he does not as yet accept responsibility for his actions" (1956, 135). The next lesson for him is to discover his own body (no. 15). ". . . We have the first mention of his penis, of its size and of his manner of carrying it in a box on his back. And for the first time are we made aware of his sexuality" (1956, 136).

In stories 19–20, Trickster decides that he would eat better if he were to transform himself into a woman and marry a chief's son. Yet his change of sex only proves that he "has as yet developed no sense of true sex differentiation" (1956, 137).

He begins to long for security, and he goes home (no. 22). But the wanderlust dies hard, and he has still not settled down for good. He says to himself, "I used to wander around the world in peace. Here I am just giving myself a lot of trouble." The slow transformation to maturity, morality, and responsibility is inevitable, but an element of nostalgia always remains. Trickster's wistfulness about "wandering around the world in peace" is "his protest against domestication and society with all its obligations. Doubtless this also voices the protest of all Winnebago against the same things" (1956, 140).

Radin believes that the trickster cycle represents, among other things, a satire on Winnebago society (1956, 151). The telling of the story is an outlet for the frustration the Winnebago adult feels towards the constraints of society, and in particular it is a protest against the constraints of religion and ritual. The narrator is using the trickster's voice to express the narrator's feelings (1956, 152). Radin does not mention Freud, but when the narrator uses the trickster as a sort of ventriloquist's puppet, saying what the human is not allowed to say, the process is a form of displacement, which Freud thought of as essential to humor: a bypassing of the superego in order to say what is forbidden.

Radin then summarizes his discoveries in order to determine where and when the trickster figure began. ". . . How did the cycle in its oldest form really begin? I think it is safe to say that it began with an account of a nondescript person obsessed by hunger, by an uncontrollable urge to wander and by sexuality" (1956, 165).

If, says Radin, we trim the trickster cycle from all other tale-cycles that have overlapped it, we end up with something like the following:

> In a world that has no beginning and no end, an ageless and Priapus-like protagonist is pictured strutting across the scene, wandering restlessly from place to place, attempting, successfully and unsuccessfully, to gratify his voracious hunger and his uninhibited sexuality. Though he seems to us, and not only to us but to aboriginal peoples as well, to have no purpose, at the end of his activities a new figure is revealed to us and a new psychical reorientation and environment have come into being. . . .
>
> But what, we may ask, is the content, what is the meaning of this original plot? About this there should be little doubt, I feel. It embodies the vague memories of an archaic and primordial past, where there as yet existed no clear-cut differentiation between the divine and the non-divine. For this period Trickster is the symbol. His hunger, his sex, his wandering, these appertain neither to the gods nor to man. They belong to another realm, materially and spiritually, and that is why neither gods nor man knows precisely what to do with them. . . .
>
> And so he became and remained everything to every man—god, animal, human being, hero, buffoon, he who was before good and evil, denier, affirmer, destroyer and creator. (1956, 167–69)

Radin's remarks apply to all the tricksters—Raven, Coyote, Hare, Old Man, and so on (although none of these is solely a trickster)—as well as to the Winnebago figure. It is not the particular animal form of the trickster that defines him, but his character and his role.

The Winnebago cycle and the Raven cycle have only a few tales in common. The Winnebago story in which Trickster becomes a woman (Radin's no. 20) is undoubtedly related to "Raven Becomes a Woman" (my no. 20) and the similar Siberian tales. The child who will not be pacified (no. 21) faintly resembles an episode from "The Theft of the Sun," and the killing of the bear somewhat resembles

Raven's "The Killing of Grizzly Bear." Radin's tales 41 to 44 are all variations of "The Bungling Host." In the last story, no. 49, Trickster has his last meal on earth. He sits on top of a rock, and the imprint of his buttocks is said to be still visible. Countless local legends of Raven are likewise told in North America and Siberia, explaining the shapes of certain features of the landscape as Raven's belongings.

Radin also examines the cycle of the Assiniboine character Sitconski or Inktonmi (1956, 97–103). Many of the tales are the same as those told of the Winnebago Trickster. Others resemble Raven tales, but these particular stories are not really trickster tales. The cycle begins, for example, with "The Earth Diver," with muskrat successfully diving for earth. Then we are told that the earth is covered with snow, because a medicine man keeps the summer tied up in a bag. Inktonmi must distract the medicine man while the summer is stolen and passed to a relay of animals. "The Theft of Summer" is a rather uncommon story in North America, related to "The Theft of Fire" and "The Theft of the Sun."

Raven actually shares his trickster stories more frequently with other Northwest Coast trickster-transformers, such as Mink or Blue Jay (Boas [1916] 1970, 585–86), than with such geographically distant characters as the Winnebago Trickster or Sitconski. But even between Raven and the Winnebago Trickster one can see a resemblance. The trickster is characterized by (among other things) an urge to wander, by gluttony and lust, by a childish lack of self-awareness, by a breaking of all rules of behavior, and by malicious tricks that often backfire, and Raven shares all these traits.

THE AUSTRALIAN CROW

Remarkable similarities can be found between the tales of the Northwest Coast Raven and the tales of the Australian Crow. The Australian tales suggest that there is a common primeval substratum to the myths of many cultures, a set of elemental ideas.

The tribes of southeastern Australia consist of two moieties (divisions), Crow and Eagle (*Aquila audax*, also known as the eaglehawk), recalling the moieties of the Tlingit and Haida. Like the Northwest Coast Raven, the Crow is a totemistic figure; Frazer notes that a member of the Crow moiety cannot kill crows (1950b, 799). The Australian mythical crow, like the North American Raven, is a thief and a trickster, surviving on his wits. The Australian Crow is also, like Raven, a transformer, giving certain animals their present appearance. He is usually turned from white to black by fire; the blackening is usually a punishment. He is not much of a culture hero, although in the Pleiades story below he seems to be a Prometheus figure gone wrong. Unlike the North American Raven, the Australian Crow does not appear as a creator, but this aspect is rare in North America anyway. As in North America, the mythical events take place in a former time (in Australia called the Dreamtime), when the characters have both human and animal form.

A story like Raven's "Theft of Fire" occurs in Victoria. It survives in several versions, but its general form is somewhat as follows. The seven sisters of the Pleiades are the only ones to have the knowledge of fire, which they keep in the end of their digging sticks. The crow pretends to be their friend so he can discover their secret. He shows them a termite nest. They dig into it to get the termites, but out come some snakes that the crow has hidden there. They hit the snakes with their sticks. The fire falls out, and the crow steals it. The crow later refuses to share the fire with anybody. He chases people off and throws coals at them. The coals start a brush fire, and he is caught in it and burned to death. The corpse turns into the bird we know as the crow (Frazer 1930, 15–19).

Frazer remarks that the significance of the digging stick may be that when it is made, it is hardened by being placed in a fire (1930, 18–19).

In another tale from Victoria, the crows own fire and will give it to no one else. The fire-tail wren sees them playing with fire-sticks, so he grabs one and runs away. He passes it to a hawk, who manages to set the whole country on fire, so now fire can be obtained from many places (Frazer 1930, 15–19).

In another tale, the punishment is emphasized. The eagle has two wives, the kestrels. He tries to train his two nephews, the crow and the magpie, in the rules of the tribe. The crow and the magpie are pure white at this time. They do not like their uncle's strict discipline, so they spear him. The wives find his body. They chant songs to bring him back to life. The eagle finds his nephews celebrating his "death," so he threatens to kill all creatures. His wives convince him to punish only the nephews. The wives cause a storm to arise, and the nephews and their friends rush to a cave for shelter. The eagle lights a fire at the entrance. The crow, who is nearest the entrance, is turned completely black, and the magpie partly so (Mountford 1969, 26).

In a story of the crane and the crow, the latter has a Raven-like obsession with food. The crane catches some fish, and the crow asks for some. The crane tells him to wait until they are cooked. The crow tries to steal one before they are cooked, so the crane hits him across the face with a fish. The crow falls onto the burned grass around the fire and is turned black (Parker [1896–98] 1978, 111).

A tale of the rivalry between the Australian crow and eagle, in which the crow kills his own nephew, ends by ascribing the crow's change of color to both lightning and punishment:

> At last the willy-wagtail got sufficient courage to look out of the camp. . . . He looked toward the west, and suddenly there was a flash of lightning out of the clear sky, and at the same time the call of the crow broke out on the still night air. Suddenly it dawned upon the eagle-hawk and the willy- wagtail that the crow had adopted the lightning as his totem. . . .
>
> Meanwhile the crow had not escaped entirely, for as a result of his visiting the earth in flashes of lightning, seeking revenge, he was burned and singed just like the colour of a dead coalfire. Thus was the crow changed in colour from pure white to black. He was punished, too, because he had slain his nephew, and instead of living half man, half bird, he was brought back to his former state. (Smith [n.d.] 1970, 52–55)

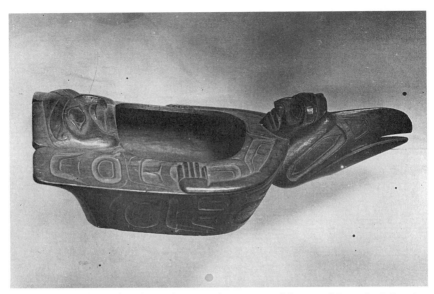

Raven grease dish (Haida). *Photograph courtesy of the Royal British Columbia Museum, Victoria, British Columbia, PN1052.*

5
THE OLD-WORLD RAVEN

MANY OLD WORLD DEITIES WERE ASSOCIATED with the raven or crow. Nergal was an important god of the Near East (originally Sumeria); at first a solar or chthonian fertility god, he became a god of the underworld, of plague, and of war, and his animal symbols were the raven, the bull, the dragon, and later the lion-griffin ("Nergal," *passim*). Ilabrat, also known as Papsukkal, was another Near Eastern god; he was the messenger of Anu and was represented on monuments by a raven (Langdon 1964, 176–77). Mithra was the god of a mystery religion, once rivalling Christianity in importance, which began in Persia but spread throughout the Roman Empire; the raven is a constant figure in the iconography and seems to be a solar figure, like Mithra himself (Keith and Carnoy 1964, 62–68, 159–60, 304–09; Hinnalls 1971, 85, 88, 210, 442; Leroy A. Campbell 1968, 22–27, 304–06). Yima (Yama, Dharmaraja) was another diety who began in Persia; originally a sun god (*Yasna* 9.4), he became a god of justice and of the dead in India, and the crow was his principal animal symbol (Shastri 1976, 423–24; Keith and Carnoy 1964, 62, 159–60, 305–06, 312–15; Crook [1926] 1972, 372). Much further east, the Japanese sun-goddess Amaterasu was represented by a giant crow (Chamberlain 1982, 169, 170).

The raven or crow appears extensively in the early religions of the

135

Germanic and Celtic peoples. Throughout Germanic and Celtic literature, the raven and wolf appear on battlefields, waiting to devour the corpses of the slain. Odin, the Norse god of war and chief of the gods, had two pet ravens and two pet wolves; the ravens kept Odin informed of what was going on in the world (Snorri Sturluson n.d., 63–64). In ancient Ireland the crow was associated with the goddess of war, whose name or epithet varied, but who was sometimes referred to as the Badb-catha, although others spoke of three war-goddesses, Neman, Macha, and Morrigan or Morrigu; the Irish hero Cuchulain is also associated with the crow (Hennessy 1870–72, *passim*). Lug, an important Celtic sun-god represented by the raven, gave his name to Carlisle, Lyon, and other cities, and his festival, Lugnasadh (August 1), is our modern Lammas (Krappe 1931 and 1936, *passim*). The early British (Welsh) god Bran ("Raven") appears in the *Mabinogion* and in later literature.

Of the classical gods, Apollo was frequently associated with the raven, as we shall see. The Greek goddesses Athena (Ovid, *Metamorphoses* 2.542–95; Apollonius Rhodius 3.925–44) and Hera (Pausanius 4.34.6; 9.3.1–5) both had the crow as one of their symbols, and Juno, the Roman counterpart to Hera, had the crow as her symbol before she adopted the peacock (Festus, *On the Significance of Words*, s.v. *corniscarum divarum*). The crow was also a symbol of Cronos, the father of Zeus (Cook 1964, 1: 625 n.5, 626). Cronos' name probably means "Crow" rather than "Time"; a number of Greek and Roman deities and mortals were named Coronus, Coroneus, Corax, etc., all meaning "Crow" or "Raven."

Throughout the myths and folklore of the Old World, the raven is associated with the sun, the color white, and water or rain.

In one of Horace's odes (3.27), the raven is a bird of both sunrise and rain:

> For the one I love, I, all-knowing prophet,
> with prayers shall arouse
> from the rising sun the raven,

the divine bird of the threatening rain,
before he returns to the still pools.

In Britain the earliest record of the raven as a symbol of sunrise is seen in *Beowulf* 1800–02 (Hume 1969, 60). After a victory feast, Beowulf and his men sleep until dawn:

They slept
Until the black raven, the blithe-hearted,
Proclaimed the joy of heaven.

In Shakespeare's *Cymbeline* (2.2.48–49) the villain Iachimo steals a bracelet from the sleeping Imogen and then returns to his hiding place to wait for morning:

Swift, swift, you dragons of the night, that dawning
May bear the raven's eye!

Like the Old World raven, the North-American and Siberian character is also a solar figure, particularly in the sense that he is responsible for stealing the sun and putting it in the sky. Again like the Old World raven, he can be specifically a symbol of the sunrise. A common expression in Northwest Coast tales is "before the raven calls," referring to the sunrise. In a Tlingit tale, for example, a man goes to fight a sea monster and tells his wife that if he does not return "before the raven calls," he will have been killed (Swanton 1909, 166–68). Among the Tlingit and Haida, "supernatural beings went hunting or on expeditions at night and had to get ashore before the raven called; if not they would die instantly" (Swanton 1908, 452). Among the Yakutat Tlingit, "the rule is that anything dangerous, uncertain, or pertaining to the supernatural should be done or at least begun before the raven calls at dawn and before one has eaten" (De Laguna 1972, 1: 362).

In some parts of the Old World, the raven is a more general solar figure, rather than specifically a symbol of the sunrise. For example, in China:

The Emperor Ya, in the twelfth year of his reign (2346 B.C.) . . .
met a man carrying a bow and arrows. . . . . This was Ch'ih-chiang
Tzu-yu. He told the Emperor he was a skilful archer and could fly in
the air on the wings of the wind. . . . The Emperor named him Shen
I, 'the Divine Archer.'. . .

Shen I led his troops to the bank of the Hsi Ho, West River, at Li
Shan. Here he discovered that on three neighbouring peaks nine
extraordinary birds were blowing out fire and thus forming nine new
suns in the sky. Shen I shot nine arrows in succession, pierced the
birds, and immediately the nine false suns resolved themselves into
red clouds and melted away. Shen I and his soldiers found the nine
arrows stuck in nine red stones at the top of the mountain. (Werner
[1922] 1976, 180–81)

Granet identifies the birds: "Yi, the Good Archer. . . killed nine
solar Ravens and allowed only one to live; he thus preserved the
world from the danger of being scorched" (1959, 366–67). (Granet
also notes that the appearance of several suns in the sky is a frequent
theme in Chinese legend and usually denotes disaster, specifically
political revolution.)

In ancient Chinese art, the sun is usually represented by a raven,
the "Red Bird" or "Golden Bird." The sun represents the male
principle, *yang*, odd in number, and so the solar raven is said to have
three legs (Charles A. S. Williams 1974, 102–3, 378). The earliest
literary allusion to the Chinese three-legged raven dates from 314
B.C. (Aston 1972, 115 n.3). Amaterasu, the chief deity of Shinto
(pre-Buddhist) Japan, was a sun-goddess represented by a giant crow,
yata-garasu (Chamberlain 1982, 169, 170). In a Chinese-Japanese
dictionary of the tenth century, the Chinese solar crow, *yang-wu*, is
identified with the Japanese *yata-garasu* (Aston 1972, 115 n.3).

Most Old World gods associated with the raven are solar gods.
Amaterasu and the Persian Yima are solar deities represented by the
crow. The raven of Roman Mithraism is depicted in art as flying from
the sun towards Mithra, himself considered the *sol invictus*, the
"invincible sun." Apollo was mainly identified with Helios, the sun,
in late Roman times, but even in Hesiod's *Theogony*, written in the

eighth century B.C., he is referred to as Phoebus, "Shining." Apollo's raven was white, perhaps therefore a solar bird. The Celtic raven-god Lug is a solar deity with a bright face and long hands (Krappe 1931, *passim*).

The Viking god Odin, "God of the Ravens," is depicted in art with the "solar wheel." His solar nature is not clearly stated in recorded myth, though both ravens and horses (another type of solar creature) are among his symbols. But Odin is described as having only one eye; among his many names are "Bileyg," "Baleyg," "One-Eyed," "Flame-Eyed." The equation of eye with sun is world-wide: for example, the Tlingit say the sun and moon are "the eyes of the sky" (Boas 1895, 320), and among the Eastern Woodland Indians "the eye of the Great Spirit" was a general term for the sun (Alexander 1964, 42); the Egyptians called the sun and moon the eyes of Horus (Müller 1964, 102); the Malay term for sun is *mata hari*, literally "eye day"; and Shakespeare tells us that "the sun with one eye vieweth all the world" (*Henry VI* 1.4.84).

Fire, sometimes apparently as a substitute for the sun, plays a part in the North American tales we have been studying.

"The Theft of Fire" is ascribed to many European animals. The robin and the wren are important "fire birds" in western Europe, the swallow in eastern Europe and Asia. By bringing fire, the robin's breast was burned red, and a hole was burned in the swallow's tail (or he was burned black or red). The wren's feathers were all burned off, so he had to borrow feathers from other birds and now has a speckled plumage. In these Old World tales, as in many North American tales, fire is sometimes relayed from one animal to another.

Only a few hints of a fire-bearing crow can be seen in Europe. In a medieval Jewish tale, "a raven goes to find the water of heaven and the water of hell. The latter is so hot that the bird was burnt." And Edlinger reports that "because of his shining plumage the raven [*Steinkrähe*] also became known among us as the 'fire raven' [Feuerrabe]" (Rooth 1962, 221).

Why should the raven be a symbol of the sun? Perhaps partly because where ravens are common, they "announce the dawn."

Eliade, however, has a stronger explanation. He points out that many (perhaps most) peoples regard God as "the one on high," "the one above," "our Father who art in heaven" (Eliade 1958, 38–111). Because God is "on high," other things "on high" are also regarded as sacred. Sun, moon, planets, stars, rain, and lightning appear in the symbolism of many religions, and the birds that fly "on high" are also symbols of a god or gods. The Christian God takes the form of a dove, Zeus and Indra take the form of eagles, while a Celtic or Germanic god is more likely to take the form of a raven. Birds fly between heaven and earth; they are "messengers" of the gods. The soul, flying up to heaven, is commonly depicted as a bird. Shamans dress in bird costumes or "become" birds in order to fly to the spirit world.

The second mythical raven to consider is the white raven. The raven is almost universally described as having originally been white. In North America and eastern Siberia, a common explanation for the crow's change of color is the tale of "The Painting of the Birds." Other common explanations in North America, eastern Asia, and Australia are part of various tales involving sun and fire. Some of the Chukchi say that Raven was turned black by the fire from the sun, moon, and stars he released. Some of the Tlingit say he was trans- formed by smoke. The Pawnee and the Cherokee say the crow was turned black by trying to steal fire (according to the Pawnee, from the sun), and the Yurok say the raven successfully stole fire from the sun, though they do not mention his change of color. In Australia, the crow is commonly said to have been turned black by fire.

There are a greater variety of explanations in the western Old World. *Leucos corax*, "white raven," was an ancient Greek term for "something rare," corresponding to Juvenal's *corvo rarior albo* (7.202), the Italian *corvo biancho*, and the German *weisser Rabe*. According to Aristotle (1965, 3.519a12),

> seasonal conditions, such as unusually sharp frost, cause some birds whose plumage is of a single colour to change. Thus, those with dark or darkish plumage turn white, e.g., the raven, the sparrow, and the

swallow, though no instance of a white bird changing to black has been observed.

A god, apparently Apollo, told the Boeotian people of Greece to settle wherever they saw white ravens. Some children scattered chalk on ravens that were flying around the Pagasitic Hill, and so the Boeotians built a city there, which they named Korakas, "Ravens" (Photius, *Lexicon*, s.v. *es korakas*).

Ovid offers two explanations for the raven's change of color, both related to Apollo. In one story, he tells us that Apollo once took Coronis ("Crow") as his lover. But Apollo's white raven brought him the news that she was being unfaithful. He killed Coronis, and then cursed the raven for inducing him to kill her and turned the raven from white to black (*Metamorphoses* 2.531–47, 596–632).

According to another of Ovid's tales, Apollo once prepared a feast for Jupiter. He gave his white raven a golden cup and told it to fetch some water. The raven flew away, but it saw some unripe figs. It waited until they were ripe and ate a few before returning to its master. The raven claimed that a serpent had been denying it access to the spring. Apollo knew the bird had been lying, and so he turned it from white to black. The story, according to Ovid, illustrates the fact that the constellations Corvus, Hydra, and Crater (Raven, Water Serpent, and Cup) appear together in the sky (*Fasti* 2.243–66).

In India, it is said that Raja Chanaka asked the crows to go to Yama and discover what lay in store for his soul. The crows returned and told him to go down the Narbada in a white boat with black sails. When the sails became white, he would know that he had reached Suklatirtha ("Bright Place of Pilgrimage"), and his soul would be saved. Yama was so angry at the Raja's escape from hell that he passed all his sins onto the crows and turned them from white to black (Crooke 1926, 372).

According to one Arabic tale, Mohammed once hid from his enemies in a cave, and a white crow discovered him and cried *ghar! ghar!* ("cave! cave!"). Mohammed's enemies did not understand the bird, but when Mohammed left the cave he punished the crow by

Silkscreen depicting Raven stealing the sun, by Ken Mowatt. *Photograph courtesy of the Royal British Columbia Museum, Victoria, British Columbia, CPN14355.*

turning him black and by making him and his descendants continue to cry *ghar! ghar!* (Rowland 1978, 37).

An Estonian tale also explains the raven's change of color in terms of sin:

> The raven was once snow-white. When the first young maidens lost their chastity and their sense of shame, the raven likewise lost his white feathers and became black. Only under his left wing did the raven retain one white feather. Whoever can acquire this feather is the luckiest man on earth, since with this feather he can get anything he desires, and he can live forever. (Dähnhardt [1907–12] 1970, 3: 517)

In Austria, the crow's transformation is probably due to deluge tradition:

> A hero once killed an unclean spirit and his lover. He cut up their bodies and scattered them over a wide field. A raven and a crow came by and began to devour their corpses. The raven ate only from the devil, and so his whole body became black. The crow, however, is white and black, since he ate from the devil as well as his lover. (Dähnhardt [1907–12] 1970, 3: 59)

In France, the crow's sin is merely intoxication, and the transformation recalls the soot of "The Painting of the Birds":

> In olden times the hooded crow was completely white and remained with us in summer as well as in winter. Once he drank too much in a tavern. He could no longer find the door and finally fell into a coal box belonging to the innkeeper's wife. He ended up greyish black, and his color has remained so since that time. Shortly after the incident he met God, who asked him: "Why do you have this color?" The crow told him without the slightest hesitation. Then the Lord said: "Since you have so shamelessly drowned your senses, you shall have no summer, but only winter." Since then the hooded crow has left our area in summer, to fly to colder countries. (Dähnhardt [1907–12] 1970, 3: 258)

An example from Hungary bears a resemblance to the Arabic tale, but with a different interpretation of the crow's voice:

> The raven was previously white and lived on clean food. When Jesus fled from his persecutors, the raven saw that they could not catch him, and he cried *kar!* ["pity!" or "harm!"]. Jesus cursed him, so that he became black and had to feed on carrion. (Dähnhardt [1907–12] 1970, 2: 51)

In the Tirol, the crow commits a different transgression against Jesus:

> The ravens and crows were once snow-white and quite beautiful proud birds. They lived by a little brook and bathed in it. One day the child Jesus was very thirsty and wanted to drink from the brook. But the ravens sat in the water and kept muddying it. Then said the child Jesus: "Since you are so unthankful and so proud of your blindingly white plumage, until the end of the world you shall have black feathers." Since then ravens have been black. (Dähnhardt [1907–12] 1970, 2: 77)

Almost everywhere in Europe and the Near East, the crow's transformation is related to punishment; many further examples can be found in Dähnhardt. Most often it is the deluge that provides the framework for the story, and his crime is either his failure to return to the ark or his consumption of corpses.

The crow's change of color is partly pseudo-etiology, an explanation of "how things came to be," like the story of "how the bear lost his tail" (it got stuck in the ice, thanks to the fox). But white animals, including albinos, are often regarded as sacred. The northern Athapaskans believe that each type of animal has a "master" or "boss," a white animal (Martin 1978, 171). The Blackfoot speak of a white beaver, "the chief of all the beavers" (Grinnell [1892] 1962, 119). The eastern culture-hero Manabhozo, the Great Hare, is said to be white (Thompson 1929, 11; Radin 1956, 74), and so is the Siberian Hare (Bogoras 1902, 658).

The white animal might also be a solar symbol. Frazer notes that the Angoni of Africa "sacrifice a black ox for rain and a white one for fine weather," and that in a Japanese rain-making ritual "custom has prescribed that . . . the colour of the victim shall be black, as an emblem of the wished-for rain-clouds. But if fine weather is wanted, the victim must be white, without a spot" (Frazer 1950b, 84). Among the Blackfoot, "if a white buffalo was killed, the robe was always given to the Sun. It belonged to him" (Grinnell [1892] 1962, 258). Such data, applied to the crow, however, would constitute only an argument by analogy.

As we have seen, the raven is almost universally regarded as a solar symbol. However, although the white raven is also a universal figure, in Europe he is apparently not regarded as equivalent to the solar raven, except in the sense that the white raven is associated with solar gods. It is only in the eastern Old World (and, of course, in the New World) that the two are clearly regarded as equivalent: the Chukchi raven is turned from white to black by stealing the sun, the Australian crow is turned black by fire, and in China a red or golden raven represents the sun.

In the Old World and the New World, a number of birds are regarded as harbingers of rain, particularly the woodpecker and certain waterfowl, but the crows are certainly the most popular rain-birds. The North American Raven steals water from the weather-god Ganuk to sprinkle it (to rain?) on the land, thereby creating rivers. The Judeo-Christian deluge myth maintains the association of ravens with rain.

According to Pliny, if a raven utters a continuous gurgling sound and shakes itself, it indicates a storm is on the way; if the call terminates with a swallowing or gulping sound, the rain will arrive in gusts (*Natural History* 18.87.362–63). Horace's raven, as we have seen, was also the *imbrium divina avis imminentum*, "the divine bird of the threatening rain." Virgil tells us that we can expect rain when we hear the voice of the raven or when we see flocks of crows deserting their feeding grounds (*Georgics* 1.382–88). Lucretius claims that crows and ravens change their voices in order to call for either rain or wind (ll. 1083–86).

According to Theophrastus:

> It is a sign of rain if the raven, who is accustomed to make many different sounds, repeats one of these twice quickly and makes a whirring sound and shakes his wings. So too if, during a rainy season, he utters many different sounds, or if he searches for lice perched on an olive-tree. And if, whether in fair or wet weather, he imitates, as it were, with his voice, falling drops, it is a sign of rain. (1949, 16)

According to Aratus, ravens indicate good weather when they call two or three times late in the day, or when they flock to roost in greater numbers than usual (*Phenomena* 949–1003).

The inhabitants of Crannon in Greece had a sacred bronze carriage, which they shook while praying for rain. Bronze coins from Crannon of the fourth century B.C. show the carriage bearing an amphora. One or two ravens perch on the wheels. The same scene was depicted on the coat of arms of the city (Cook 1964, 2: 831–33). Frazer suggests that the shaking of the carriage was meant to imitate thunder (1922, 309). Perhaps the amphora held water. A similar wheeled vessel was found much further north in Skallerup, south Jutland (Davidson 1967, pl. 21).

Ovid's myth of the raven who brought a cup of water to Apollo also seems to have the rain as its underlying symbol, to judge from a slightly different account by Aelian:

> All through summer the Raven is afflicted with a parching thirst, and with his croaking (so they say) declares his punishment. And the reason they give is this. Being a servant he was sent out by Apollo to fetch water. He came to a field of corn, tall but still green, and waited till it should ripen, as he wanted to nibble the wheat: to his master's orders he paid no heed. On that account in the driest season of the year he is punished with thirst. (1958: 1.47)

In every European country today, it is said that "crows indicate

rain." In Norwich, England, jackdaws indicate rain if they perch on
the vanes of church towers (Swainson 1886, 81):

> *When three daws are seen on Saint Peter's vane together,*
> *Then we're sure to have bad weather.*

In France, "when the rook (or raven) flies low, he carries ice under
his wing; when he flies high, he bears warm weather" (Swainson
1886, 87).

The Italian "thirsty crow" must drink from the sky:

> When, at the beginning of the world, the Lord had created springs
> for all animals and creatures, he excepted only the raven. "You may
> not drink from the springs, but only from the water that falls from
> the sky. You must catch it out of the air with your beak." When it
> rains, these creatures stand with their beaks open, and they observe
> the weather, to see if it will rain. So when the raven croaks, go home;
> it will rain soon. (Dähnhardt [1907–12] 1970, 3: 322)

One possible reason why crows are rain symbols is that they leave
many countries in the summer and head north, only returning
during the winter, the season of rain. This is more true of the smaller
species, however, than of the raven. In Britain (Swainson 1886, 87)
it is said that

> *On the first of March*
> *The caws begin to search:*
> *By the first of April*
> *They are sitting still:*
> *By the first o' May*
> *They're a' flown away!*
> *Croupin' greedy back again,*
> *Wi' October's wind and rain.*

The rain symbolism is repeated in China. Edward Armstrong
(1958, 86–87) refers to a Chinese legend in which "a raven flies

through the woods causing a storm and so warning creatures that the gods are about to ride past." The fifteenth story of the Mongolian *Siddhikur* tells of a crow who shows a thirsty prince where to find water (Busk 1873, 158).

In *The Manciple's Tale* (ll. 299–301), Chaucer retells Ovid's story of Apollo and Coronis, with a few interesting changes. After killing Coronis, Apollo curses the crow:

> *You and your offspring shall always be black,*
> *And never sweet sounds shall you make,*
> *But always cry before storm and rain. . . .*

How did the raven become a symbol of rain? Perhaps ravens and other crows really do act differently before it rains. Ornithologists regard crows as among the most intelligent of birds, and their behavior, particularly their "vocabulary," is certainly complex. It is a common saying that "birds fly low before a storm," and one still hears of weather-signs specifically related to the crows. It is also likely that the crow's black plumage makes him a rain-symbol. In many cultures, rain is represented by the color black, sun by the color white. While the biological black crow is a rain symbol, the mythical white (or red) crow is a solar symbol. Again, Eliade's remark about things "on high" being sacred is probably relevant. There are several possible answers one can give to the questions of the raven's symbolism. This probably means, not that one or more of the answers are false, but rather the reverse: it may be *because* the raven can be tied into such a complex web of symbols and meanings that he became such a popular figure.

The pluvial raven and the solar raven are not entirely opposite. We tend to think of sun and rain in contrast to each other, but what is more relevant is that rain and sun are both part of the sky, and the sky is associated with a great many gods throughout the world. The raven belongs to the sky; in other words, he is also regarded as divine.

6

THE SHAMANIC RAVEN

FASCINATING MAGICAL AND RELIGIOUS ELEMENTS appear in the raven myths of the Old World and the New, in particular, various intricate relationships between the raven figure and the practices of shamanism. According to Eliade, shamanism is "preeminently a religious phenomenon of Siberia and Central Asia" (1976, 4). Shamanism includes the following elements:

(1) One may inherit shamanic powers, or certain highly sensitive individuals may feel a "calling." Usually to become a shaman one must "die," be visited by spirits, have one's body be transformed, and be "reborn."

(2) The shaman is able to undergo a trance or "ecstasy" in which his soul is carried (he "flies") to the world of the spirits, which may be in the sky or underground. There he gains knowledge and power from the spirits. He also learns "the language of animals," and he may imitate their sounds during his seance.

(3) The shaman communicates with two types of spirits, "familiar" and "tutelary." The "familiar" spirit usually takes animal form. The "tutelary" spirit is usually "the soul of a dead shaman or a minor celestial spirit" (Eliade 1976, 90). The shaman may also communicate with the gods or semi-divine beings worshiped by the general community.

(4) The shaman has the gifts of precognition and clairvoyance. He can also ensure a plentiful supply of game, control the weather, and cure illness. Curing illness may involve travelling to the spirit world in order to recapture the patient's soul. He can not only cure; he can also use supernatural means to cause illness or death.

(5) The shamanic conception of the universe includes several different levels of heaven, as well as a Cosmic Axis, the center of the Universe, which may take the form of a tree, pillar, mountain, or (less often) a bridge or ladder.

(6) The shaman's costume gives him animal form.

> The three chief types are that of the bird, the reindeer (stag), and the bear—but especially the bird. . . . Feathers are mentioned more or less everywhere in the descriptions of shamanic costumes. More significantly, the very structure of the costumes seeks to imitate as faithfully as possible the shape of a bird. . . .

In most of Siberia, the dominant mythic and shamanic figure is the eagle.

> The eagle . . . , held to be the father of the first shaman, plays a considerable role in the shaman's initiation, and, finally, is at the centre of the mythical complex that includes the World Tree and the shaman's ecstatic journey. Nor must we forget that the eagle in a manner represents the Supreme Being, even if in a strongly solarized form. (Eliade 1976, 156–58)

In easternmost Siberia and North America, however, the raven replaces the eagle as the principal shamanic figure. The Koryak Big-Raven "set up shamans to struggle with evil spirits. . . . He is invisibly present at every shamanic performance" (Jochelson 1904, 417).

> When the shamans of the Maritime Koryak commence their incantations, they say, "There, Big-Raven is coming!" The Reindeer Koryak told me that during shamanistic ceremonies a raven or a sea-gull comes flying into the house, and that the host will then say,

"Slaughter a reindeer, Big-Raven is coming!" I had no opportunity to witness personally any sacrificial offering to Big-Raven; but at the fawn festival, which is now observed only by the Reindeer Koryak of the Palpal Mountains, the antlers piled up during the festival constitute a sacrifice to Big-Raven. (Jochelson 1908, 18)

A large number of Koryak Raven tales are satires on shamanism, as we shall see in the next chapter.

Raven also founded shamanism among the Tlingit: "There was a man who had no arm, so Raven thought he would be a shaman and cure him. This is how the Tlingit came to have shamans" (Swanton 1970, 84).

Boas has recorded some details from the Kwakiutl:

When it is desired that the owner of an after-birth should understand the cries of the raven, the after-birth is put down on the beach where the ravens peck at it. And when it is pecked at by the ravens, the man, when he is full grown, will understand the cries of the raven, for the people of olden times considered it important that the raven came to report about the arrival of warriors who came to make war upon the tribes. Then they would come at once and ask one who understands the raven, tumbling about and crying. It is bad news when they are tumbling about and feathers fall out. (Boas 1913, 606)

The raven was a divinatory figure for the Blackfoot:

The raven has the power of giving people far sight. It was also useful in another way. Often, in going to war, a man would get a raven's skin and stuff the head and neck, and tie it to the hair of the head behind. If a man wearing such a skin got near the enemy without knowing it, the skin would give him warning by tapping him on the back with its bill. Then he would know that the enemy was near, and would hide. If a raven flew over a lodge, or a number of lodges, and cried, and then was joined by other ravens, all flying over the camp and crying, it was a sure sign that during the day some one would come and tell the news from afar. (Grinnell [1892] 1962, 261)

The North American raven's "divinatory" powers are partly related to hunting. Grinnell records a Blackfoot belief that "the ravens often told the people that game was near, calling to the hunter and then flying a little way, and then coming back, and again calling and flying toward the game" ([1892] 1962, 261). According to Lopez, "The Nunamiut Eskimo . . . believe . . . that perhaps wolves learn from the behavior of ravens where caribou might be" (1978, 3). Such beliefs may have some basis in fact; it is known that ravens commonly associate with wolves, and that they travel with wolves on the hunt, sometimes flying ahead of the pack (Mech 1970, 287–88).

Echoes of the raven or crow's divinatory ability can be found in many parts of the western Old World as well (Best 1911 *passim*; Owen [1896] 1977, 314–16; Pollard 1977, 127–28; Crooke 1896, 1: 166, 2: 48–49, 243–45; Westermark 1926, 268, 463, 331–33). In general, good or bad fortune is determined by the number of crows seen (usually an even number is good luck), or by whether a single crow appears on the left or the right; the latter belief may have some relation to the directions of the sunrise and sunset (Brown 1936, 274). In Scotland, to have "the raven's knowledge" is to possess supernatural insight (John F. Campbell [1890] 1970, 1: 285). In the Hebrides, it is said that if a boy drinks out of a raven's skull, he can locate dead bodies (Armstrong 1958, 78).

The crow is regarded as "the wisest of animals" by the Blackfoot (Grinnell [1892] 1962, 101, 110; McClintock 1910, 483); the same belief is held in India (Ryder 1956, 307), and Chaucer mentions "the raven wise" in *The Parliament of Fowls* (l. 363). In Rome, Greece, India, and Ireland, he is often regarded as "the oldest of animals" (Plutarch, *On the Obsolescence of Oracles* 415 C 11; Ovid, *Metamorphoses* 7.179–293; Shastri 1976, 424–25; Crooke 1926, 371; O'Sullivan 1966, 15–18). Age and wisdom are almost always associated in folk tradition.

According to ornithologists, crows are possibly the most intelligent of birds, so folklore is partly in accordance with science in terms of the question of the crow's wisdom. However, although ravens may be "the oldest of animals" in a mythical sense, the popular belief that ravens live to a great age is not correct; the lifespan of birds is related to their size, and ravens (or other crows) are no exception to this rule (Pettingill 1967, 399–400; Goodwin 1976, 61). The belief that the raven is "the wisest of animals" and "the oldest of animals" is probably derived from his divinity or sacredness. In the late Middle Ages, the crow became largely a figure of evil, but this attribute is also possibly an indication of his divinity. Many devils were originally gods, and the Latin word *sacer* means both "holy" and "evil."

Among Old World deities, the Greco-Roman Apollo and the Norse Odin possess striking shamanic qualities.

Apollo, god of music, medicine, and prophecy, was associated with the dolphin, mouse, hawk, falcon, swan, wolf, ass, and (mythical) griffin. But, as we have seen before, his principal animal symbol was the raven. The relationship between the raven and Apollo might be explained by Apollo's origins. He was primarily the god of the Hyperboreans, those people whose name apparently means "Beyond the North Wind." But where did the Hyperboreans live? According to Hecateus, they lived on a very large island (Britain?) near the coast of Gaul (Diodorus Siculus 2.47). Pindar says that Hercules visited the Hyperboreans and then brought back the olive from the Ister (Danube) (*Olympian Odes* 3.26–30). The olive does not grow on the shores of the Danube, but the region itself might be significant. Herodotus claims that "sacred gifts" were brought by the Hyperboreans to Scythia (north of the Black Sea), and from there they were transported to the island of Delos in the Aegean (4.33.1–4). Other authors give various—though always vague—descriptions of the locations of the Hyperboreans, but the consensus seems to indicate a northern origin for these people, as their name suggests.

Further evidence for a northern origin for Apollo lies in the resemblance between Siberian shamanism and the cult of Apollo. According to Eliade, "the few figures of Greek legend who can be compared to shamanism are related to Apollo" (1976, 388). Herodotus (4.13–18) tells of the poet Aristeas, from the island of Proconessus, in the Sea of Marmara (northeast of Greece). One day Aristeas supposedly died, but when his relatives went to claim the

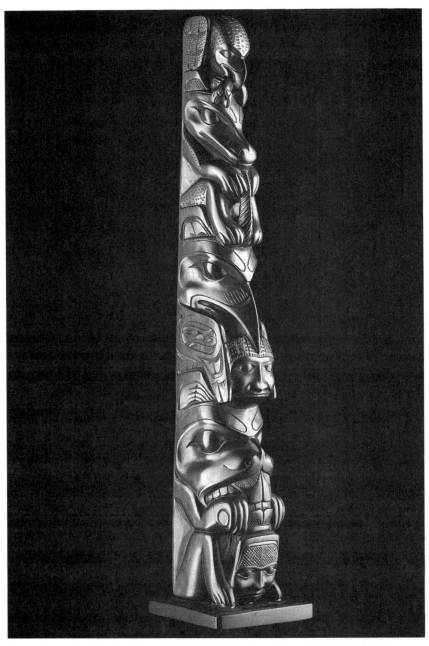

Slate totem pole. *Photograph courtesy of the Royal British Columbia Museum, Victoria, British Columbia, CPN6105.*

body, it had disappeared. Seven years later, Aristeas reappeared on Proconessus, and again disappeared. Two hundred and forty years later, a man appeared in Metapontum in Italy. He claimed to be Aristeas, and he told the inhabitants that they were the only people to whom Apollo had ever appeared, and that he himself had accompanied Apollo at that time, taking the form of a raven.

A similar figure is Abaris, also a disciple of Apollo. He carried a golden arrow, or flew through the air on it, and he could cure illness and predict disasters. A magic arrow often appears in shamanic tales (Eliade 1976, 388).

The tales of Aristeas and Abaris have (separately or together) much in common with Siberian shamanism, including the magical flight, the raven, the magic arrow, and the ability to cure disease. William Guthrie concludes that Apollo "came to the Greeks from an original home in the north-east, perhaps Siberia" (1950, 204).

The tales of Odin have even more in common with Siberian shamanism. Odin's name means "fury," "mental intoxication," "ecstasy" (Davidson 1981, 70, 147), recalling the shamanic ecstasy or trance. Like a shaman, he "could transform his shape: his body would lie as if dead, or asleep; but then he would be in the shape of a fish, or worm, or bird, or beast, and be off in a twinkling to distant lands upon his own or other people's business" (Snorri Sturluson 1951, 11).

Odin was the chief of the Norse gods, and he was the god of war—or more specifically, of dead warriors, whom he called to join him in Valhalla, his home. Odin had a long beard and only one eye. The other eye had been given as a payment for drinking from the spring of the giant Mimir, which flowed from the World Tree Yggdrasil ("Steed of Odin") and was said to give wisdom. Odin had an eight-legged horse, Sleipnir; the *Heimskringla* (Snorri Sturluson 1951, 97) mentions the consumption of horseflesh at a feast dedicated to Odin. He also had two other kinds of animals:

He gives what food he has on his table to two wolves called Geri [Greedy] and Freki [Gluttonous]; but he himself needs nothing to eat. Wine is for him both food and drink. . . . Two ravens sit on his shoulders and bring to his ears all the news that they see and hear; they are called Hugin [Thought] and Munin [Memory]. He sends them out at daylight to fly over the whole world, and they come back at breakfast-time; by this means he comes to know a great deal about what is going on, and on account of this men call him the god-of-the-ravens. (Snorri Sturluson n.d., 63–64)

"Olaf Tryggvason's Saga" (in the *Heimskringla*) tells the story of Hakon the Great, who had been converted to Christianity against his will. He travelled to Sweden and held a sacrifice to Odin. Two ravens flew overhead and called to him, and so Hakon knew that he was still in Odin's favor (Puhvel 1973, 244).

Odin's World Tree, Yggdrasil, has branches that spread out over the entire world, and its three roots reach to the three regions of the universe. The sacred tree, the center of the world, is a major symbol of Siberian shamanism, though of course there are other parallels, including the Tree of Life in Genesis.

The eight-legged horse also appears in Siberia:

According to a Buryat legend, a young woman takes as her second husband the ancestral spirit of a shaman, and after this mystical marriage one of the mares in her stud gives birth to a foal with eight legs. The earthly husband cuts off four of them. The woman cries: "Alas! it was my little horse on which I used to ride like a shamaness!" and vanishes, flying through the air, to settle in another village. She later became a guardian spirit of the Buryat. (Eliade 1976, 469)

Divination often entails learning "the language of animals," sometimes specifically "the language of crows." Porphyry notes that the Etruscans understood the language of eagles, the Arabs that of ravens (*On Abstinence* 3.4). Philostratus claims that the Arabs learned the language of birds by eating the hearts or livers of snakes (*Life of Apollonius of Tyana* 1.20).

The language of animals, as a general motif, is found throughout world folklore. The power may be gained by the acquisition of a magic ring, or by the acquisition of a magic plant, particularly fern seed (which also confers invisibility). But most often it is a serpent that grants this power. The serpent may lick the hero's ears, or the hero may eat the heart or liver of a (usually white) serpent (Frazer 1950a, 93–127). Quite frequently the language that the hero learns is that of crows.

The *Volsunga-Saga* tells of Sigurd, who once dug a hole, hid himself in it, and killed the serpent Fafnir as he passed over it. He roasted the serpent's heart. When he touched the heart to see if it was cooked, he burned his finger. He put his finger to his mouth and instantly understood the language of birds; he heard the nuthatches speaking on the branches.

Snorri Sturluson, in his *Heimskringla*, says that King Olaf Kyrre once heard of an old serf who could predict the future and who knew the language of birds. The king ordered the serf's horse to be secretly killed and brought on board his ship, and then had the serf brought to him. The serf was ordered to act as a pilot and row before the king's ship. A one-year-old crow flew overhead, calling loudly, and the serf listened. A two-year-old crow also flew overhead, calling even more loudly, and the serf's hands grew weak. Then a three-year-old crow flew overhead. The oars dropped from the serf's hands, and he turned to the king, who asked him what they were saying. The serf replied that the birds were saying that the king had killed the horse and brought it on board the ship. King Olaf was so struck by the serf's abilities that he gave him the legal title to the land he worked, and he also gave him many other fine gifts (Snorri Sturluson 1951, 247–48).

According to a Buryat tale (Coxwell 1925, 148),

> An orphan lad, who lay beneath a tree,
> Observed alone some crows in converse free.
> He heard, "The khan's young son is weak and ill;
> His friends a barren, piebald mare should kill
> And place her hide over the child in pain;
> His sickness would depart, he'd breathe again."

Even the Grimms' tales have some interesting crow lore: in "Faithful John," for example, the faithful servant sees three ravens flying overhead; he can hear the birds talking to each other, predicting three disasters and describing how to prevent them.

So the raven of European religion and folklore is generally shamanic. He takes on certain supernatural attributes reminiscent of shamanism: he is an indicator of the weather (not a trivial subject to hunting and agricultural peoples before our own day); he is a figure of divination, particularly in terms of the language of animals; and he symbolizes good and evil in human fate. He is also a symbol or messenger of various anthropomorphic gods, particularly the northern shamanic gods Odin and Apollo.

It is a truism that primitive cultures have animal gods, that civilized cultures have anthropomorphic gods, and that in Egyptian culture one can see the transition: the gods are depicted with human bodies but animal heads. When a god is anthropomorphized, the animal figure does not always disappear, but may remain as a symbol, a "pet," or a messenger of the god. The raven, then, may once have been a god himself, but in historical times he merely appears as a companion of a god.

There are other birds, of course, who play important roles in myth and folklore. The wren, for example, hunted and killed at the winter solstice, had a place in Celtic religion. The woodpecker was a rain-bird and an occasional symbol of Mars and Zeus. But the crow's principal rival or parallel is the eagle. Eagle, bull, and lion dominate the art and literature of the great civilizations (Mesopotamia, Egypt, Crete, and the Indus Valley) which began to arise in the third millenium B.C. So it is likely that the eagle of European myths represents a fairly late intrusion from the Near East, the birthplace of western civilization (Armstrong 1958, 130–38). It is also worth noting that in spite of the importance of eagle's feathers in North American ritual, the eagle plays only a minor role in North American myths.

If we allow ourselves to indulge even further in speculation, we can consider the possibility that certain myths reflect the intrusion of the mythical eagle into regions where the mythical raven once predominated. In Greek myth, Zeus, the eagle, deposes his father Cronos, the crow. The soul of King Arthur, a Celtic figure, is said to inhabit a raven (or another black bird, a chough or puffin), and it is said that he is imprisoned in a cave guarded by eagles (Armstrong 1958, 131).

This intrusion theory might explain why the raven is the major figure in Celtic and Germanic lands, as well as in easternmost Siberia, while in between, in central Asia, the eagle is the dominant figure. The shamanism and myths of central Asia were heavily influenced by southern cultures, and the eagle may have been part of that influence.

Raven hat (Tlingit). *Photograph courtesy of the National Museums of Canada/Canadian Museum of Civilization, 102990.*

Raven rattle. *Photograph courtesy of the Royal Ontario Museum, Toronto,* HN903.

7
SOME
THEORIES

SEVERAL SCHOLARS HAVE TRIED TO UNRAVEL THE mysteries of the Raven tales. Waldemar Bogoras and Waldemar Jochelson studied the relationship between the North American myths and the Siberian ones. Paul Radin was primarily concerned with the relationship between the trickster and the creator, and with the sociological aspects of the trickster figure. Elizar Meletinsky's areas of concern are very much like those of Radin, but the emphasis is on the Siberian figure. But G. S. Kirk and Stith Thompson have presented some general concepts about myths and folktales which may help to clarify the Raven tales, and it is with their theories that we shall begin.

MYTHOLOGY AND METHODOLOGY

In order to effectively analyze the Raven tales, we should consider them in the wider context of the general study of myths. A good starting point might be the first few chapters of G. S. Kirk's *The Nature of Greek Myths,* a masterpiece of clarity and conciseness. His essential point is that the study of myths has been hampered by the attempt to dominate the subject with what he calls "monolithic theories": theories that may or may not be valid, but that apply, at best, only to certain kinds of myths, and do not serve to explain all kinds of myths.

> Myths . . . constitute an enormously complex and at the same time indefinite category, and one must be free to apply to them any of a whole set of possible forms of analysis and classification. . . . Myths . . . are often multifunctional, and consequently different hearers can value a myth for different reasons. Like any tale, a myth may have different emphases or levels of meaning. . . . Analysis of a myth should not stop when one particular theoretical explanation has been applied and found productive. (1974, 38–39)

There are several kinds of monolithic theories, and Kirk begins with those that claim that "myths refer primarily to the world of nature or to men as involved in society or worshipping gods," as opposed to theories that see myths as born primarily within the human psyche (1974, 69).

(1) ". . . All myths are *nature myths*, that is, they refer to meteorological and cosmological phenomena. Originally a German obsession, [the theory] spread to England and reached its climax under Max Müller . . ." (1974, 43).

(2) "Second . . . is the one loosely covered by the term *aetiological*; it implies that all myths offer a cause or explanation of something in the real world. . . . It suggests that myths were a kind of halting advance on the road to epistemological maturity" (1974, 53).

(3) "Malinowsky . . . proposed . . . that [myths] should be considered as *charters* for customs, institutions, or beliefs. By that he meant something close to 'explanations' in a loose sense, but devoid of theoretical quality" (1974, 59). Myths are seen as "a validation of traditional customs, beliefs and attitudes" (1974, 32).

(4) Mircea Eliade's belief is that "the purpose of all myths is to evoke, or actually to re-establish in some sense, the *creative era*. . . . By reconstituting that era one can also revive some of its unique creative power. Any tale that restores for a time the mythical past is helping the world to . . . share in the power of the divine actions *in*

illo tempore. . . . Australian myths are especially relevant here, since it is a common Aboriginal idea that the beings that existed at the beginnings of the world still exist. They live on in a disembodied form in what is called by some tribes the 'Dreaming Era' or 'Eternal Dreamtime' . . ." (1974, 64–65).

(5) ". . . Myths are closely associated with rituals. In its extreme form [the theory] asserts that myths are actually derived from rituals. . . . Functionalists saw society as a tight and complex mechanism, every aspect of which was related to basic social ends (marriage, property, the rules of kinship). Rituals were a prominent aspect of savage societies, among others; myths therefore must be fitted into the same pattern" (1974, 66–67).

Kirk then examines "a group of interpretations that claims to find the ultimate reality of myths in the individual psyche itself" (1974, 69). He includes the theories of Freud, Jung, and Lévi-Strauss in this class.

In *The Interpretation of Dreams*, "Freud recognized that myths and dreams often work in the same way" (Kirk 1974, 71). In both cases, the functions of the unconscious are those of "condensing the material of daytime experience, displacing its elements, and representing it in symbols and images" (Kirk 1974, 72).

Jung, on the other hand, saw myths and dreams "as revelations of what he called the 'collective unconscious', an inherited and continuing involvement of mankind with certain key symbols" (Kirk 1974, 77), which he called "archetypes."

Finally, Kirk interprets Lévi-Strauss as saying that

the structural unity of the social machine is effected by the consistent structure of the minds that ultimately determine its forms. . . . Lévi-Strauss can even tell us one of the main characteristics of this structure: a tendency to polarize experience, to divide it for the purposes of understanding into sets of opposites, much as a binary computer does. (1974, 81)

According to Kirk, none of the above theories can explain all the Greek myths, or all the Tsimshian myths, or all of the myths of

Africa, let alone all the myths of the entire world. At best, any one of the above theories may explain a few myths, but no monolithic theory can explain all myths. There are simply too many different kinds of things that myths are made of.

Stith Thompson claims that folktales (which, in a primitive culture, are the same as myths [Boas (1940) 1982, 406]) can be seen as built up from basic elements, which he calls *motifs*. Motifs may be actors ("witches, ogres, fairies . . . cruel stepmothers"), background objects ("magic objects, unusual customs, strange beliefs, and the like"), or—most commonly—single incidents (1977, 415–17). A specific group of motifs, in a specific sequence, constitutes what he calls a *tale-type*.

Thompson describes what is called the "historical-geographical method" for studying folktales. One first assembles all the known variants of a tale and analyzes them into individual traits. Then, by looking at each trait's frequency of occurrence, the extent of its distribution, its striking qualities, its naturalness and essentialness, and so on, one should be able to finally trace the history and geography of the entire tale (1977, 430–44).

Thompson's method seems to be useful in answering a very important question: If two tales in two different parts of the world resemble each other, should we say that these tales evolved separately in the two cultures, or are we dealing with a single tale that was brought (or taught) by one culture to the other? This question is sometimes regarded as one of "independent origination" versus "diffusion." Thompson would apparently say that if we can show that in both cultures we are dealing with the same tale-type (i.e., the same motifs in the same sequence), then we are dealing with a case of diffusion.

A problem can arise with the historical-geographical method, however: What is one to do with tales that consist of a single motif (as is so often the case with the Raven tales)? Thompson admits that the method "cannot be successfully employed unless the tale is present in a relatively large number of versions—the more the better—and unless the tale has enough complexity to permit a

breaking up into separate traits which can be studied independently."
And yet, "all depends on how simple the motif is. . . . Where there is
variation, there is the possibility of study by this method" (1977,
439–40).

The immediate relevance of Thompson's work to the Raven tales
is that if we wish to trace their historical or geographical origins, we
cannot rely on a vague similarity between the tales of any two
cultures. If we wish to say that a tale in one area is the same as one in
another area, we must be prepared to prove that in both cases we are
dealing with the same tale-type, i.e., the same motifs in the same
order.

THE TRICKSTER-CREATOR DICHOTOMY

In chapter 4, we looked at Radin's general remarks on the nature of
the trickster, but we should also consider his theories on the nature
of Raven in particular. They seem to consist of two main points:
   (1) The Raven tales are just a minor form of trickster tales.
   (2) The trickster was only later (and clumsily) converted into a
deity. The difference between Haida and Tlingit forms of "The Birth
of Raven" illustrates this transition.

In almost all versions of the trickster cycle in North America, there
are episodes describing the creation of the earth, or the transformation of the world into its present shape and with its present plants
and animals. The main character in these creation and transformation stories is a wanderer, obsessed with hunger and sexual desire. He
has no conception of ordinary human morality, and he employs
deception and duplicity to gain what he wants. Quite frequently, he
fails to attain his goals, he becomes a victim of his own traps, and he
ends up as a target of ridicule. How the creation elements enter the
overall story of the trickster is the puzzle Radin sets out to solve
(1956, 155).

Radin devotes a lot of attention to the question of whether the
trickster is a deity lately demoted to the rank of buffoon, or whether
he is fundamentally a clown who only in later times became clumsily

elevated to the role of deity. He seems to find it self-evident that the present-day (i.e., non-prehistoric) Raven tales are basically trickster tales, even though his own figures leave one in doubt:

> To form some idea of the proportion of episodes relating to origins as compared to those of the purely trickster type, let me give some figures. On the North-west Coast there are seventeen of the former out of forty-five; among the Blackfoot, five out of twenty-six; among the Gros Ventre, three out of twenty-six; among the Assiniboine, five out of fifty-two; among the Menominee, three out of twenty-seven; among the Shoshone, five out of thirty-six; and among the Crow, five out of twenty-eight. (1956, 167)

He attempts to prove that the trickster was not originally a deity, and he derives his evidence from stories of the trickster's early life. Radin uses the Raven stories for much of the evidence for these theories. Disregarding Boas' elaborate division of "The Birth of Raven" (Boas [1916] 1970, 621–36) into Tlingit, Haida, and Tsimshian-Kwakiutl types, and so on, Radin concentrates on one issue. He claims that virtually all the Indian groups that recount the Raven tales begin in one of two ways. Some peoples describe a world that is originally covered (or largely covered) with water, and Raven's birth is not described, because he (like all true tricksters) is regarded as having always existed. Others describe the world as cloaked in darkness, and then Raven's birth is described, with Raven regarded as the son or nephew of a god.

Radin then gives Haida and Tlingit versions of these stories. In the Haida story, Raven is in a world that seems to be nearly all water. He flies about, looking for a place to sit, then goes on various adventures (Swanton 1905, 110–12). In the Tlingit story, on the other hand, the world "at the beginning of things" is covered in darkness, and Raven-at-the-head-of-the-Nass lives with his sister, who gives birth to Raven himself (Swanton 1909, 81–82).

> If we compare these two types of introduction it is difficult to escape the conviction that in the case of the Tlingit we are dealing

with a secondary accretion, and that the Haida is much closer in form to the true beginning of the trickster myths. In the Tlingit myth there is a complete break between Trickster conceived of as a divine being and as a transformer of the world and the Trickster whose actions have no purpose and who behaves like a fool. (Radin 1956, 159–60)

Presumably what Radin means is that the Tlingit have created Raven-at-the-Head-of-the-Nass as an attempt to turn Raven the trickster into a god, and that they have left the nephew of Raven-at-the-Head-of-the-Nass to fulfill the original trickster role.

Radin then mentions similar Gros Ventre, Blackfoot, and Crow myths with "the same break between Trickster conceived of as a divine being and as a buffoon" (1956, 162). Regarding the frequent use of "The Earth Diver" as an opening story among these tribes, Radin remarks:

> . . . It seems fairly certain that the original cycle did not begin in this manner, that this opening belongs to an entirely different cycle, either to that relating to the typical culture-hero and the transformer of the world, as illustrated by the Winnebago *Twin, Red Horn,* and *Hare Cycles* . . . or to specific origin myths.
>
> That, originally at least, Trickster was not a deity in the ordinary sense of the term seems evident. That attempts were constantly being made to elevate him to such a rank is, however, equally clear. (1956, 162–64)

Radin uses the Tsimshian version of "The Birth of Raven" as another example of this deification process: a son dies, but one day the mother goes to visit the corpse and she finds a youth, shining like fire. The woman adopts the youth, and her husband gives him a "raven-blanket" and tells him to fly to the mainland and scatter fruit and fish roe over the world.

> Thus we see here, too, the attempt to give Trickster a divine pedigree is manifestly unsuccessful. . . .
>
> On the basis of all these facts only one conclusion is possible, namely, that Trickster's divinity is always secondary and that it is

largely a construction of the priest-thinker, of a remodeller. (1956, 164)

The attempt may be unsuccessful, but it is not manifestly so. I can only assume that what Radin means is that an element of grandiosity has been added, by means of the boy's physical appearance, the adoption into the chief's family, the gifts, and so on, all of which contrast with the derogatory description of the trickster at the beginning of the Winnebago cycle.

There are problems with the Tlingit and Haida stories that Radin uses as evidence of Raven's "late" elevation to the position of deity. In the first place, Radin claims that stories in which Raven is described as being born (e.g., the Tlingit story) are evidence that a trickster figure is being split into two figures, a deity and a trickster, yet one could just as easily claim the opposite: that Raven, like many deities, originally had a mother and father, and that his trickster role was a later accretion. Secondly, the Haida story that Radin refers to is hardly a simple story of a trickster about to start out on a series of pranks: the story, in fact, continues with the account of how Raven took two stones, threw them into the sea, and thereby created two worlds, the Queen Charlotte islands (the home of the Haida) and the mainland.

Elizar Meletinsky's 1959 paper on the Siberian raven figure covers a wide range of theories:

(1) "Whatever is common in the folklore of Asia and North America must be the most ancient" (1959, 87). What is most common is the culture-hero and creator tales, not the purely trickster tales (tales in which Raven is mainly a rogue or glutton).

(2) "... The Chukchi myths of Raven as culture-hero are the most ancient element of the Raven tales ..." (1959, 92). Meletinsky bases his belief partly on the fact that Raven is "almost never portrayed as a coastal dweller" (1959, 89), even though the Chukchi are now composed of Maritime (coastal) and Reindeer (inland) groups. Hence "the Raven tales [have] purely Paleo-Asiatic roots going back to the time when the Paleo-Asiatic peoples of the Chukotsky group

were not yet divided into 'coastal' and 'hunter [reindeer]' groups . . ."
(1959, 90).

Meletinsky thinks he can identify a "primordial core of the 'Raven'
myths," consisting of "Raven's abduction of light from its keepers,
the obtaining of fresh water and the creation of rivers, and the
receiving of good weather. Also, the story of how Raven painted
other birds while he changed color from white to black, how Raven
created the first people and how he created reindeer, fish, and beasts
for them as food" (1959, 93–94). Sometimes Raven's accomplishments as a culture-hero are disguised. They become inverted, and
they are thereby treated as the pranks of a trickster. While in the
original myth, Raven obtains the sun for mankind, in the Koryak
inversion, Raven-Man swallows the sun, and Big-Raven's daughter
has to coerce him into spitting it out (1959, 93, 97). When he creates
dogs and people out of garbage, the tale is a parody on Raven's role
as creator (1959, 98).

(3) The origin tales are the same on both sides of the Bering Strait;
the trickster tales differ in several respects (1959, 94). Raven's gluttony is treated quite differently in Asia and North America:

> Among the north-west Indians the different stories of Raven's cultural
> activities or tricks were becoming elements of his biography. A desire
> to comprehend the contradiction between Raven as culture-hero and
> Raven as trickster brought about the creation of the story of how
> Raven became gluttonous, which he did by eating scabs from bones.
> (1959, 94)

The Siberian view of his hunger is based on economics:

> The driving force pushing Raven to perform his tricks is hunger. . . .
> However, while Indian folklore treats Raven's gluttony as a disease in
> its own right (the result of his eating scabs from a bone), Koryak
> folklore explains this largely by hunger due to a shortage of
> provisions. . . . This picture of hunger . . . is a reflection of the severe
> conditions of the struggle for existence in the extreme north-east of
> Asia. (1959, 96)

Most North American stories of Raven's birth do not appear in Siberia:

> As a rather late fruit of the cyclization of the Raven tales among the Indians, the story about his birth and childhood appeared. Events such as the competition between uncle and nephew, the origin of Raven from the "mistress of the surf" (according to one version), and other events from Raven's childhood have a specific Indian character, reflecting certain aspects particular to the folklore and ethnography of the north-west Indians (for example, the transfer of power along the mother's side etc.).
>
> The cyclization of the Raven tales in the folklore of the Koryak and Itelmen [Kamchadale] took on a different character. Neither the Koryak nor the Itelmen know the stories about Raven's birth. On the other hand they know various adventures of Raven's sons and daughters, and also stories about the relationship between Raven and his wife Miti. (1959, 94)

(4) Raven might have been a totemistic ancestor, as suggested by stories of rivalry with other birds. The stories may, to some extent, represent friendly rivalry between members of different phratries. Raven was sometimes called "Big Grandfather," and he appears as a totem ancestor of one of two phratries among the Ngasam Yakut (1959, 90).

(5) The trickster tales are a form of satire, serving as an outlet for the rebellious feelings of the story-teller and the audience (1959, 99). Raven's gluttony and sexual infidelity are the themes of the tales. Yet at the end of each tale, the social norms are upheld (1959, 95).

> . . . All the . . . methods Raven used to obtain food are of a particularly unearned, and even parasitical, character. . . . one cannot justify Raven's egotistical yearning to hide food he has obtained from his own family, nor Raven's breaking of the rules of hospitality. . . . It is not surprising that in such stories Raven is usually unmasked and shamed. . . . All Raven's attempts to be unfaithful to Miti . . . end in failure. (1959, 96)

... When ... the paradoxical behavior of Raven acquires an obvious asocial character, violating the norms of morality, or trying to corrupt human nature, the folktale mercilessly makes fun of him and dethrones him, describing the failure of his intentions. Only when morality or human nature are not affected does the folktale perceive the mischievousness and dissoluteness with encouraging, good-willed humor. (1959, 99)

(6) Some of the satire has shamanism as its target. Stories of Raven's "death" parody the shamanic death or trance, during which the shaman goes to visit the spirit world. Stories of Raven's change of sex, ostensibly in order to escape from his wife or to marry into a richer family, are a parody on the homosexuality and transvestitism that are common in shamanism; shamans are even believed to change their sex. In one story, Raven climbs into a storehouse full of food, and his wife's brother uses shamanic techniques to find the lost Raven. Shamanic techniques of healing are satirized in a tale in which Raven "revives" a hare by putting back on it the very skin that Raven had originally torn off. And finally, the shaman's supposed ability to change the weather is satirized in Raven's attempts to affect the weather by dealing with various deities in charge of wind and rain (1959, 98).

(7) There are three kinds of Raven tales: origin tales, trickster tales, and hero tales. The first two types have been noted by many scholars, and are clearly delineated by native narrators, but Meletinsky speaks of a third type of tale, the heroic. Hero tales of Raven are not very common; they are in an embryonic state. Tales of this type are related to the traditional European folktales. The hero is strong, virtuous, and admirable. The role of the father of the hero is to provide support for the son. In these hero tales, Raven is the patriarch, and his son Ememqut is the hero and main character (1959, 101).

Meletinsky is not always cautious with his data or his conclusions. We are told in a brief footnote that "it is highly likely that originally Raven and the 'Creator' (Tenantogan) were one and the same person" (1959, 91 n. 16). Such a statement sweeps Radin's entire

"The Raven and the First Men," carving by Bill Reid, 1970 (Haida).
Photograph courtesy of W. McLennan, UBC Museum of Anthropology.

book-length theory under the carpet, and yet Meletinsky offers little solid evidence for his own belief. He mentions Radin's book (*The Trickster*), so it is not as if he were unaware that there are alternatives to his own theory. When he writes that "myths about the obtaining of fire . . . are unknown to the Paleo-Asiatic peoples" (1959, 94), he is not entirely accurate: the "Theft of Fire" story usually found in North America does not appear in Siberia, but Bogoras and Jochelson both mention that Raven showed people how to use the fire-drill. Meletinsky also claims that the "plot about the breaking of a hole in the firmament" ("The Wall of Dawn") is unknown in North America (1959, 94), and yet it was known at least to the Bella Coola (Boas 1895, 241).

His broader statements are also open to doubt. In the first theory listed above, he says that "whatever is common in the folklore of Asia and North America must be the most ancient" (1959, 87), and yet one might suggest that whatever is common to both continents is simply whatever is most attractive: a story might be widespread for the sole reason that it is unusually funny, for example, not because it is unusually old. Yet Meletinsky's further explanations tend to give his statement some plausibility: he goes on to explain that most of the origin tales are common to both continents, whereas the trickster tales have salient differences in their general framework. So in general terms, Meletinsky's statement makes sense, even if it is not correct with respect to some specific tales.

The second theory, that the strictly inland setting of the Chukchi Raven culture-hero tales proves that they date to before the Chukchi separated into inland and coastal groups, is to some extent circular, because he seems to be saying: the culture-hero tales are the most ancient; the Chukchi tales are mostly culture-hero tales; so they are the most ancient. It is only if we accept, in the first place, that culture-hero tales are older than trickster tales that the circularity disappears.

Meletinsky analyzes the Raven cycle in two other interesting essays, published in 1973 and 1980, although again there are problems, including several minor inaccuracies, such as the statement (1980, 101) that the Lillooet are an Athapaskan tribe of the southeastern United States. He claims (1973, 114), citing Lévi-Strauss, that the Indians ascribed the raven's harsh voice to his suffering from thirst, whereas this folk belief is widespread in Europe and rarely if ever found in North America (Dähnhardt [1907–12] 1970, 3: 364–75). He also endorses (1980, 126) Lévi-Strauss's theory that the raven and coyote were chosen as tricksters because they are scavengers and hence "mediators" between carnivores and herbivores (yet what does one do, for example, with Hare, who is the eastern equivalent to Raven and yet a complete herbivore?). We are told (1980, 121) that "the central heroic myth of Tlingit folklore," i.e., "the struggle between Iel and Naschakiel," "apparently has no parallel among the Athapaskans," and yet the Tahltan version of this myth is very similar to that of the Tlingit (Teit 1919, 198–200). Meletinsky concludes his 1980 paper by saying (1980, 125; cf. 108) that the "original bearers of [North American] Raven myths" must have been speakers of Na-Dene languages (Tlingit, Haida, and Athapaskan), yet he offers no evidence; he is merely jumping at the obvious, whereas Boas points out ([1940] 1982, 427) that the spread of myths in North America is more a matter of geographic contiguity than of linguistic affiliation.

HISTORICAL AND GEOGRAPHICAL ORIGINS

When and where did the Raven tales begin? It is quite safe to say that the tales are derived from both Old World and New World traditions, but the relative importance of each tradition is less clear.

Actually, when we look for an origin for a tale, we must realize that there is no such thing as a distinct and isolated origin for any of the tales. It is more a case of following each tale backwards from one time and place to another until the tale becomes too amorphous to be worth following any more—or simply until the trail goes cold.

"The Theft of the Sun" may be genetically related to the Old World conception of the raven as a solar figure, although the absence of a very similar tale in the Old World (west of Bogoras' line) makes the relationship hard to prove. The tale is not even closely matched by any other North American myth, although that of Coyote is somewhat similar.

In Northwest Coast art, Raven is shown with the sun in his beak. The iconography is ambiguous; a figure with a sun in its mouth appears in art or literature from Egypt to Siberia, but it is usually a figure that swallows the sun, rather than releasing it. It is puzzling that the North American figure is said to represent quite the opposite. In the Koryak tale, for example, Raven takes the sun *out* of the sky and swallows it; the "swallowing of the sun" element reappears in other Old World myths. In the Ainu tale we looked at in chapter 3, the devil tries to swallow the sun, and a crow flies down the devil's throat to stop him. The southern Slavs have a tale of a werewolf who swallows the sun (MacCulloch and Máchal 1964, 229), and in Norse tradition it is said that the wolf Fenrir will swallow the sun when the world comes to an end (Snorri Sturluson n.d., 86). Okladnikov (1959, 44), speaking of the art of eastern Siberia early in the first millennium B.C., mentions "a large, isolated figure of a mythical monster, trying to swallow some kind of a round object. It is possible that this drawing represents the monster Mongus, which is well known in the myths of Central Asia, trying to swallow the moon or even the sun." It is tempting to suggest that the "sun-swallowing" motif is derived from a northern culture familiar with the long winter night, but in Egyptian myth the god Seth is forced to regurgitate the sun he has swallowed (Müller 1964, 127, 401).

"The Theft of Fresh Water" seems to be derived from the Old World conception of the raven as a water bearer and as a harbinger of rain, though the resemblance is far from precise.

"The Earth Diver" and "The Deluge" are so clearly recognizable in motif and sequence across so many cultures, including those of surpassing antiquity, that an Old World origin seems certain. The former may be from India, while "The Deluge" is Semitic in origin.

It may be that the raven's appearance in "The Earth Diver" is simply a late intrusion based on the raven of "The Deluge."

"The Painting of the Birds" may be from eastern Asia. Its geographic scope in North America does not coincide neatly with the rest of the Raven tales: it is largely an Eskimo tale, and the eastern Eskimo, at least, have no tales belonging to the standard "Raven cycle."

The Malay and Vietnamese stories that resemble "The Painting of the Birds" are problematic. Is "The Painting of the Birds" an Old World tale? It is hard to believe the opposite: that a North American Indian story reached down into Vietnam. Or is the resemblance to "The Painting of the Birds" only superficial?

The Lapp and Orochi versions of "The Bungling Host" also raise interesting questions. Can we say that the Lapp and Orochi tales are trickster stories that wandered west from the Bering Strait? Or are they vestiges of Old World trickster stories that later reached the New World? Or are they not trickster stories at all, but merely tales that superficially resemble North American ones? Thompson, in fact, lists the Lapp story as a "tale-type" (no. 247*), while the North American "Bungling Host" is a separate entity and only listed as a "motif" (J2425)—but Thompson himself admits (1977, 423) that his classifications are not meant to reflect genetic relationships.

And if we have found one or two examples of "The Painting of the Birds" and "The Bungling Host" well west or southwest of the Bering Strait, would a more careful search of the literature reveal other recordings of these tales far from North America?

Hoebel (1941, *passim*) has proven that "War with the South Wind" is derived from a very similar and widespread Asian tale, "The Wandering Animals and Objects." On the other hand, "Raven Travels with His Slave" is so dependent on the chief-and-speaker relationship that it must have been invented within the highly stratified society of the Northwest Coast.

In spite of the fact that we can find an Asian origin for one or two trickster tales, Raven the *trickster* seems to have a largely North American origin. Radin shows that the trickster (using the term in the strict sense, as he has outlined it) is a fairly uniform figure over most of North America. Raven's "North American trickster" nature can be seen mainly in his overall role, his family resemblance to other tricksters or semi-tricksters, rather than in individual stories. To the extent that Raven is a trickster, the origin of the Raven tales is the same as the origin of the trickster tales. The trickster tales are so widespread and so well-developed throughout North America that it is at least tempting to think of them as largely North American in their evolution—although it is still possible that the trickster (again, using the word in the strict sense) was originally an Old World figure.

The origin tales, particularly "The Theft of the Sun," are another matter. Raven is far from being a pure trickster: the Raven tales have a much greater proportion of origin tales than is usual for North American tricksters. This is a point made by Radin (1956, 167), but he does not elaborate on it, perhaps because it tends to work against his own theory. Raven was a North American trickster, but he was also something else: a creator, a demiurge. Many of the origin tales seem to have evolved in the Old World. The general view of the raven as a creator, as a sacred or divine figure, may be related to the fact that a dozen anthropomorphic Old World gods have the raven as their pet or messenger. Chowning (1962, 3), citing Lantis (1947, 93), thinks the deification of the raven may be due to an Eskimo tendency to emphasize bird-symbolism in their myths and rituals. But there are enough raven gods all over the Old World that one does not have to assume that the Eskimo are the only possible source.

The question of whether Raven was first a creator or first a trickster can be answered in several different ways. In the first place, it is not a question of time but of place; to judge from the few tales that we have been able to trace back to their prehistoric roots, the creator Raven may be largely Old World in origin, and the trickster Raven New World in origin.

And yet one should not look for too much of a god in Raven's past. Raven only occasionally appears as a creator, and even then he may be distinguished from the Supreme Being. The Supreme Being is an obscure figure throughout North American Indian myths, and the distinction between Supreme Being and creator is also unclear, even when such a distinction may be said to exist. The creator-trickster situation may have been as vague to the Indians and Siberians of a thousand years ago as it seems to scholars of today. The Siberian and North American Raven, in other words, never was much of a god, in early times or in later times—and neither was any other Siberian or North American character.

Supreme Beings and creators are vague and shadowy beings, providing little material for stories, and their activities were not the sort of thing that these people liked to speculate on. Thompson notes that "the teachings of American Indian mythology concerning the Creator and the establishment of the universe, particularly of the earth, are, for the great majority of the tribes, fragmentary and meager and such explanations are often entirely lacking" (1977, 312). We do not usually find a description of the creation of the world *ex nihilo.* "Sometimes, but rarely, a real attempt is given to account for creation; but more often these origin tales are nothing more than reports of important changes taking place in an already existing world" (1977, 303).

For example, the Koryak often refer to Big-Raven as "Creator," but he only barely deserves this name; in most stories, he is a trickster, and he is always regarded as inferior to the Supreme Being, who is himself poorly defined. According to Jochelson, "though occupying the most important place in the religious life of the Koryak, the conception of the Supreme Being is vague. . . . The Supreme Being plays no active part in mythology . . ." (1908, 23, 26). Elsewhere he says that "the Supreme Being is represented as an old man. . . . He is, as a rule, rather inert" (1904, 417).

This pair of Ravens, the trickster and the creator, calls to mind other pairs in the tales. The Koryak have two ravens, Big-Raven and Raven-Man, and the Tlingit also have two ravens, Raven himself and his uncle Raven-at-the-Head-of-the-Nass. Chowning (n.d., 114) points out that in Nelson's study of the Bering Strait Eskimo, there are actually three ravens: the "Raven Father," who made the earth; the transformer, particularly the orphan boy who puts the sun in the sky; and the trickster, who appears in a number of tales—and one could even add a fourth, since tales such as "The Painting of the Birds" also appear in western Alaska, and in those cases the raven is definitely a bird-like character (as he is in most other Eskimo stories), not a human-like trickster. Even Afanasief's Russian folktales have a frequently occurring character called Raven son of Raven, but his adventures are thoroughly European.

There is one more pair of Ravens in North America: the Kwakiutl have a character named Omeatl ("Creator"), whose adventures are the basic Raven tales, and who flies around in a "raven cape," and yet one of his tales is "The Painting of the Birds," in which he paints the raven. We cannot say in this case that the Kwakiutl split a creator-cum-trickster raven into two figures, or that the neighbors of the Kwakiutl merged the two Kwakiutl characters. All that happened is that two traditions happened to collide: (1) the tales of Omeatl, a typical Northwest Coast transformer-trickster, who became identified with Raven, a similar figure, and (2) the Eskimo tales of a more bird-like Raven, of which "The Painting of the Birds" is by far the most popular and most widespread.

The creator-trickster dichotomy may reflect this pairing phenomenon on a larger scale: one tradition, that of a sacred creator Raven, overlaps another, that of a secular trickster Raven.

In terms of geographic origins, it is probably significant that both the biological raven and the mythical raven are largely northern figures. The biological raven is certainly a dominant figure in the northern landscape, as anyone who has been up north will attest, although it is true that ravens were at one time more common in southern regions: Shakespeare frequently mentions them, and they were often seen in Athens in Aristotle's day. The mythical raven is likewise a northern figure: he is a major symbol of Odin, chief of the Scandinavian gods, and of Apollo, apparently a northern figure, as well as the major mythical figure of the regions east and west of the Bering Strait. It is tempting to think that, in terms of the sacred aspects of the raven, Siberia formed a link between North America and the western Old World.

Perhaps the loon was a figure in those same ancient Siberian myths: we have already seen him (or her) as Raven's mother in the Tlingit "Birth of Raven," as the main character in other forms of "The Earth Diver," and as the second character in "The Painting of the Birds."

Everywhere, the raven is a fire figure or a solar figure, and (sometimes for that reason) he is said to have once been white. He is a symbol of the gods, a shamanic figure, and a figure of divination in general. We cannot always trace specific Raven tales, historically and geographically, when they consist of a single motif. Many of these motifs are worldwide in distribution, or at least very widespread. A comparison of the Northwest Coast Raven tales to the Australian Crow tales shows us that there is a common ancient substratum to the myths of so many cultures, a set of universal motifs. Just as a very early stone chopping-tool in Africa resembles one from Europe or North America, so the ancient mythical motifs from one continent resemble those of another. The half-human animal figure, the sacred white animal, the intricate solar symbolism, the theft of fire, the identification of the animal symbol with the god, and so on—these are all mythical symbols so old and so diffuse that we can never hope to find their geographic or chronological origins. They entered the New World at some untraceably early date and then emerged as parts of the Raven tales, the Hare tales, the Coyote tales, and so on. Nor should we trouble ourselves with the question of whether the universality of these primeval motifs can be ascribed to the "similarity of human minds," or to cultural diffusion; over the course of thousands of years both factors must have been important.

THE SOCIOLOGICAL ASPECTS
OF THE TALES

Meletinsky gives a good summary of the sociological aspects of Raven's "atrocious" behavior as a trickster:

Raven's tricks fail not only when they are associated with the breakdown of collective distribution and social norms in general (including hospitality), but also when they contravene physical norms, as with his wish to be of the other sex (usually for exactly the same reason as before—to establish contact with the rich reindeer breeders), or when he disregards the conventional division of labour between the sexes. (1973, 124)

And a few pages later:

> In stories of the "animal tale" category, in which Raven contests with Fox, Wolf and other "wild beasts" . . . the predominant aspect is quite patently that of the clown and trickster ready to stoop to any depths of craft and deceit to have his hunger sated. But the "tricks" of the gluttonous Raven work only if they are directed against "foreigners" (evil spirits, wild animals dwelling in other parts, the rich . . . . reindeer breeders); they miscarry, however, on any occasion when they would be to the detriment of "their own interests", if their object is to desert Miti in favour of contacts with the reindeer breeders, or to gain food merely for himself. . . . The tricks also end in failure if they involve the violation of natural physical norms . . . or the social norms. . . . (1973, 152–53)

There is considerable agreement over the sociological nature of the trickster myths. Both Radin and Meletinsky, for example, see them as reflecting concerns with social norms, although the form of reflection can vary between two extremes: on the one hand, the tales can be expressions of rebellion against the constrictions of society (Freud's theory of humor was somewhat similar), and on the other hand they can be validations of the social norms. The two extremes fit within the boundaries of the rule that "the good (or at least charming) guys always win." When Raven is being especially immoral, he loses, but if he is just being a loveable scoundrel, he may be allowed to win. Scoundrels have a certain ambivalent appeal; we can identify and empathize with them, but only if they are not about to destroy the fabric of society. Raven's villainy is mainly on the same level as Falstaff's ("I do begin to perceive that I am made an ass").

Although he was not primarily concerned with the trickster,

Raven house post (Haida). *Photograph courtesy of the Royal British Columbia Museum, Victoria, British Columbia, PN130.*

Meletinsky's theories are often more specific than Radin's. Meletinsky examines the satirical aspects very astutely. The satire is primarily in the form of inversion: the Koryak sun tale, for example, is told backwards, with Raven taking the sun *from* the sky rather than arduously winning it to put it *in* the sky. Raven's violations of social norms are also primarily inversions: his outrages are the opposite of accepted behavior.

In Siberia, the satire is often directed against shamanism, an aspect of Siberian culture for which one can imagine an emotional release (through humor) being necessary: shamans have great power over people, perhaps even frightening power, since they can both cause and cure illness and death. They perform their duties by means of magic, which may be regarded as real, or may be regarded as fraudulent tricks. In either case, it is quite apropos for Raven to be using absurd tricks of his own as he plays shaman.

Works Cited

Aelian.

1958. *On the Characteristics of Animals*. Trans. A. F. Scholfield. Loeb Classical Library. London: William Heinemann.

Afanasief, A. N.

1945. *Russian Folk Tales*. Norbert Guterman. New York: Pantheon.

Alexander, Hartley Burr.

1964. *North American. The Mythology of All Races*, vol. 10. New York: Cooper Square.

Andrade, Manuel J.

1931. *Quileute Texts*. New York: Columbia U P.

Aristophanes.

1950. *Aristophanes*. 2 vols. Trans. Benjamin Binkley Rogers. Loeb Classical Library. London: William Heinemann.

Aristotle.

1965. *History of Animals*. Trans. A. L. Peck. Loeb Classical Library. London: William Heinemann.

Armstrong, Edward A.

1958. *The Folklore of Birds: An Enquiry into the Origin and Distribution of Some Magico-Religious Traditions*. London: Collins.

Aston, William G., trans.

1972. *Nihongi*. Rutland, VT: Charles E. Tuttle.

Batchelor, Rev. John.

n.d. *The Ainu of Japan: The Religion, Superstitions, and General History of the Hairy Aborigines of Japan*. New York: Fleming H. Revel.

Bell, James Mackintosh.

1903. "The Fireside Stories of the Chippwyans." *Journal of American Folk-Lore*, 16, 61: 73–83.

Best, Richard I.

1911. "Prognostications from the Raven and the Wren." *Eriu* 8: 120–26.

Birket-Smith, Kaj, and De Laguna, Frederica.

1938. *The Eyak Indians of the Copper River Delta, Alaska.* Copenhagen: Levin & Munksgaard.

Blackwood, B.

1929. "Tales of the Chippewa Indians." *Folk-Lore* 40: 315– 44.

Boas, Franz.

1888. *The Central Eskimo.* 6th Annual Report of the Bureau of American Ethnology, 399–675.

1895. *Indianische Sagen von der nord-pacifischen Küste Amerikas.* Berlin: A. Asher.

1913. "Ethnology of the Kwakiutl." 35th Annual Report of the Bureau of American Ethnology, part 1.

1916. *Tsimshian Mythology.* New York: Johnson Reprint, 1970.

1932. *Bella Bella Tales.* Memoirs of the American Folk- Lore Society 19.

1940. *Race, Language, and Culture.* Chicago: U of Chicago P., 1982.

Bogoras, Waldemar Germanovitch.

1902. "The Folklore of Northeastern Asia, as Compared with That of Northwestern America." *American Anthropologist* New Series 4: 577–683.

1910. *Chukchee Mythology.* Rpt. from vol. 8, part 3 of the Jesup North Pacific Expedition. Leiden: Brill.

1928. "Chukchee Tales." *Journal of American Folk-Lore,* 41, 161: 297–310.

Brown, William John.

1936. *The Gods Had Wings.* London: Constable.

Busk, Rachel Harriette, trans.

1873. *Sagas from the Far East: or, Kalmouk and Mongolian Traditionary Tales.* London: Griffith and Farran.

Campbell, John Francis, ed. and trans.

1890. *Popular Tales of the West Highlands.* 4 vols. Detroit: Singing Tree Press, 1970.

Campbell, Leroy A.

1968. *Mithraic Iconography and Ideology.* Leiden: Brill.

Camsell, Charles, and C. M. Barbeau.

1915. "Loucheux Myths." *Journal of American Folk-Lore,* 249–57.

Chamberlain, Basil Hall, trans.

1982. *Kojiki: Records of Ancient Matters.* Rutland, VT: Charles E. Tuttle.

Chowning, Ann.

n.d. *Raven Myths in Northwestern North America and Northeastern Asia.* Master's thesis, U of Pennsylvania, 1952.

1962. "Raven Myths in Northwestern North America and Northeastern Asia." *Arctic Anthropology* 1, 1: 1–5.

Cook, Arthur Bernard.

1964. *Zeus: A Study in Ancient Religion.* 2 vols. New York: Biblo and Tannen.

Coxwell, Charles F., ed. and trans.

1925. *Siberian and Other Folk-Tales: Primitive Literature of the Empire of the Tsars.* London: C. W. Daniel.

Crooke, William.

1896. *The Popular Religion and Folk-Lore of Northern India.* Rev. ed. Delhi: Munshiram Manoharlal.

1926. *Religion and Folklore of Northern India.* New Delhi: S. Chand.

Dähnhardt, Oskar.

1907–12. *Natursagen: Eine Sammlung naturdeutender Sagen, Märchen, Fabeln, und Legenden.* New York: Lennox Hill, 1970.

Davidson, H. R. Ellis.

1967. *Pagan Scandinavia.* Ancient Peoples and Places 58. London: Thames and Hudson.

1981. *Gods and Myths of the Viking Age.* New York: Bell.

De Laguna, Frederica.

1972. *Under Mount Saint Elias: The History and Culture of the Yakutat Tlingit.* 3 vols. Washington: Smithsonian Institution.

Eliade, Mircea.

1958. *Patterns in Comparative Religion.* Trans. Rosemary Sheed. London: Sheed and Ward.

1976. *Shamanism: Archaic Techniques of Ecstasy.* Trans. Willard R. Trask. Bolingen Series 76. Princeton U P.

Frazer, Sir James George.

1911. *The Magic Art and the Evolution of Kings. The Golden Bough*, part 1. London: Macmillan.

1930. *Myths of the Origin of Fire*. London: Macmillan.

1950a. *Garnered Sheaves: Essays, Addresses, and Reviews*. London: Macmillan.

1950b. *The Golden Bough: A Study in Magic and Religion*. 1 vol., abridged ed. New York: Macmillan.

Gayton, A. H., and Stanley S. Newman.

1940. *Yokuts and Western Mono Myths*. Anthropological Records 5, 1. Berkeley: U of California P.

Goodwin, Derek.

1976. *Crows of the World*. Ithaca: Cornell U P.

Gould, Jennifer Chambers.

n.d. *The Iconography of the Northwest Coast Raven Rattle*. Master's thesis, U of British Columbia, 1973.

Granet, Marcel.

1959. *Danses et légendes de la Chine ancienne*. Paris: Presses universitaires de France.

Grimm, J. and W.

1960. *The Grimm's German Folk Tales*. Trans. F. P. Magoun and H. P. Krappe. Carbondale, IL: Southern Illinois U P.

Grinnell, George Bird.

1892. *Blackfoot Lodge Tales: The Story of a Prairie People*. Lincoln, NE: U of Nebraska P, 1962.

Guthrie, William K. C.

1950. *The Greeks and Their Gods*. London: Methuen.

Hatt, Gudmund.

1949. *Asiatic Influences in American Folklore*. Det Kgl. Danske Videnskabernes Selskab Historisk-Filologiske Meddelelser 31, 6.

Hennessy, W. M.

1872. "The Ancient Irish Goddess of War." *Revue celtique* 1: 32–57.

Hinnalls, J. R., ed.

1971. *Mithraic Studies*. 2 vols. Manchester: Manchester U P.

Hoebel, E. Adamson.
1941. "The Asiatic Origin of a Myth of the Northwest Coast." *Journal of American Folklore*, 54, 211–12: 1–9.

Holmberg, Uno.
1964. *Finno-Ugric and Siberian. The Mythology of All Races*, vol 4. New York: Cooper Square.

Hume, Kathryn.
1969. "The Function of the *Hrefn Blaca: Beowulf* 1801." *Modern Philology* 67: 60–63.

Jochelson, Waldemar.
1904. "The Mythology of the Koryak." *American Anthropologist* New Series 6: 413–25.
1908. *Religion and Myths of the Koryak*. Memoirs of the American Museum of Natural History, vol. 10, part 1. Rpt. from vol. 6, part 1 of the Jesup North Pacific Expedition. Leiden: Brill.

Keith, A. Berriedale, and Carnoy, Albert J.
1964. *Indian and Iranian. The Mythology of All Races*, vol. 6. New York: Cooper Square.

Kirk, G. S.
1974. *The Nature of Greek Myths*. London: Penguin.

Kleivan, Inge.
1971. *Why Is the Raven Black? An Analysis of an Eskimo Myth*. Acta Arctica, 17. Copenhagen: Munksgaard.

Krappe, Alexander H.
1931. "Lugh Lavada." *Revue archeologique* 5th series, 33: 102–06.
1936. "Les Dieux au corbeau chez les celtes." *Revue de l'histoire des religions* 114: 236–46.

Krause, Aurel.
1885. *The Tlingit Indians; Results of a Trip to the Northwest Coast of America and the Bering Straits*. Trans. Erna Gunther. Vancouver: Douglas and McIntyre, 1956.

Kroeber, Alfred L.
1908. *Gros Ventre Myths and Tales*. Anthropological Papers of the American Museum of Natural History 1: 59–61.
1976. *Yurok Myths*. Berkeley: U of California P.

Langdon, Stephen Herbert.
1964. *Semitic. The Mythology of All Races*, vol. 5. New York: Cooper Square.

Lantis, Margaret.
1947. *Alaskan Eskimo Ceremonialism*. American Ethnological Society, Monograph 11. Seattle: U of Washington P.

Liapunova, R. G.
1987. "Raven in the Folklore and Mythology of the Aleuts." *Soviet Anthropology and Archeology* 26, 1: 3–20.

Lopez, Barry
1978. *Of Wolves and Men*. New York: Scribner.

Lowie, Robert H.
1909. "Shoshone and Commanche Tales." *Journal of American Folk-Lore* 22, 85: 265–82.

McClintock, Walter.
1910. *The Old North Trail: Or, Life, Legends and Religion of the Blackfeet Indians*. London: Macmillan.

MacCulloch, John Arnott, and Máchal, Jan.
1964. *Celtic and Slavic. The Mythology of All Races*, vol. 3. New York: Cooper Square.

McKennan, Robert A.
1959. *The Upper Tanana Indians*. Yale U Publications in Anthropology 55. New Haven, CT: Yale U.

Martin, Calvin.
1978. *Keepers of the Game: Indian-Animal Relationships and the Fur Trade*. Berkeley: U of California P.

Mech, L. David.
1970. *The Wolf: The Ecology and Behavior of an Endangered Species*. Garden City, NY: Natural History.

Meletinsky, Elizar M.
1959. "Skazania o Vorone v narodov Krajnevo Severa." *Vestnik istorii mirovoj kul'tury* 1, 13: 86–104.
1973. "Typological Analysis of the Palaeo-Asiatic Raven Myths." *Acta Ethnographica Academiae Scientiarum Hungaricae 22*, 107–55.

1980. "The Epic of the Raven among the Paleoasiatics." *Diogenes* 110: 98–133.

Mooney, James.

1900. *Myths of the Cherokee.* 19th Annual Report of the Bureau of American Ethnology.

Mountford, Charles P.

1969. *The Dawn of Time.* London: Angus and Robertson.

Müller, Wilhelm Max.

1964. *Egyptian. The Mythology of All Races,* vol. 12. New York: Cooper Square.

Nelson, Edward W.

1899. *The Eskimo about Bering Strait.* 18th Annual Report of the Bureau of American Ethnology, part 1.

Okladnikov, A. P.

1959. *Ancient Population of Siberia and Its Cultures.* Russian Translation Series of the Peabody Museum of Archaeology and Ethnology, Harvard U, vol. 1, no. 1. Cambridge, MA: Peabody Museum.

Osgood, Cornelius.

1937. *The Ethnography of the Tanaina.* Yale U Publications in Anthropology 16. New Haven, CT: Yale U.

O'Sullivan, Sean.

1966. *Folktales of Ireland.* Chicago: U of Chicago P.

Owen, Elias.

1896. *Welsh Folk-Lore.* Darby, PA: Norwood, 1977.

Parker, Mrs. K. Langloh.

1896–98. *Australian Legendary Tales: Being the Two Collections Australian Legendary Tales and More Australian Legendary Tales Collected from Various Tribes.* London: Bodley Head, 1978.

Petitot, Émile.

1886. *Traditions indiennes du Canada nord-ouest. Les littératures populaires de toutes les nations,* vol. 23. Paris: G.-P. Maisonneuve et Larose.

Pettingill, Olin Sewall, Jr.

1967. *Ornithology in Laboratory and Field.* Minneapolis: Burgess.

Pollard, John.

1977. *Birds in Greek Life and Myth.* London: Thames and Hudson.

Poole, Francis.

1872. *Queen Charlotte Islands: A Narrative of Discovery and Adventure in the North Pacific.* Ed. John W. Lyndon. The Northwest Library, vol. 2. Vancouver: J. J. Douglas, 1972.

Puhvel, Martin.

1973. "The Blithe-Hearted Morning Raven in *Beowulf.*" *English Language Notes* 10, 4: 243–47.

Qvigstad, J., ed.

1927. *Lappiske eventyr og sagn.* 4 vols. Oslo: H. Aschehoug.

Radin, Paul.

1956. *The Trickster: A Study in American Indian Mythology.* New York: Schocken Books.

Rooth, Anna Birgitta.

1962. *The Raven and the Carcass: An Investigation of a Motif in the Deluge Myth in Europe, Asia, and North America.* FF Communications 186. Helsinki: Suomalainen Tiedeakatemia.

Rowland, Beryl.

1978. *Birds with Human Souls: A Guide to Bird Symbolism.* Knoxville: U of Tennessee P.

Ryder, Arthur W., trans.

1956. *The Panchatantra.* Chicago: U of Chicago P.

Shastri, H. P., trans.

1976. *The Ramayana of Valmiki.* London: Shanti Sadan.

Skeat, Walter William.

1900. *Malay Magic: Being an Introduction to the Popular Religion of the Malay Peninsula.* New York: Dover, 1967.

Smith, W. Ramsay.

n.d. *Myths and Legends of the Australian Aboriginals.* New York: Johnson Reprint, 1970.

Snorri Sturluson.

n.d. *The Prose Edda of Snorri Sturluson: Tales from Norse Mythology.* Trans. Jean I. Young. Berkeley: U of California P.

1951. *Heimskringla: The Norse King Sagas.* Trans. Samuel Laing. Rev. ed. Everyman's Library, no. 847. London: J. M. Dent.

Swainson, Rev. Charles.

1886. *The Folk Lore and Provincial Names of British Birds.* London: Folk-Lore Society.

Swanton, John Reed.

1905. *Haida Texts and Myths.* Bureau of American Ethnology, Bulletin 29.

1908. "Social Condition, Beliefs, and Linguistic Relationship of the Tlingit Indians." 26th Annual Report of the Bureau of American Ethnology 391–485.

1909. *Tlingit Myths and Texts.* Bulletin 39, Bureau of American Ethnology.

Teit, James.

1910. *The Mythology of the Thompson Indians.* Memoirs of the American Museum of Natural History. vol. 12. Rpt. from vol. 8, part 2 of the Jesup North Pacific Expedition. Leiden: Brill.

1919. "Tahltan Tales." *Journal of American Folk-Lore,* 32, 124: 198–252.

Theophrastus.

1949. *Concerning Weather Signs.* In *Enquiry into Plants and Minor Works on Odours and Weather Signs.* Trans. Sir Arthur Hort. 2 vols. Loeb Classical Library. London: William Heinemann.

Thompson, Stith.

1929. *Tales of the North American Indians.* Cambridge, MA: Harvard U P.

1971. *The Types of the Folk-Tale: Antti Arne's* Verzeichnis der Märchentypen *translated and enlarged.* FF Communications 74. Helsinki: Suomalainen Tiedeakatemia.

1977. *The Folktale.* Berkeley: U of California P.

Trevelyan, Marie.

1909. *Folk-Lore and Folk-Stories of Wales.* London: E. Stock.

Werner, Edward T. C.

1922. *Myths and Legends of China.* New York: Arno, 1976.

Westermark, Edward.
1926. *Ritual and Belief in Morocco*. London: Macmillan.
Williams, Charles A. S.
1974. *Outlines of Chinese Symbolism and Art Motives*. Rutland, VT:
Charles E. Tuttle.
Williams, Roger.
1643. *A Key into the Language of America*. Ed. John Teunissen and
Evelyn J. Hinz. Detroit: Wayne State U P, 1973.
Zheleznova, Irina, trans.
1976. *Northern Lights: Fairy Tales of the Peoples of the North*. Mos-
cow: Raduga, 1989.

Index